Welcome. It's great to have you with us.

For more than nine decades the Royal Flying Doctor Service of Australia (RFDS) and the Country Women's Association (CWA) have worked to improve life in the bush.

This publication is a joint effort between the RFDS and CWA. Our aim was to bring together stories, anecdotes, prose, artwork and recipes that talk to life in Australia's outback.

This book captures "Struth!" moments – good and bad – and provides real stories of how Aussies come together to assist each other in times of need.

We were flooded with written contributions that are as varied as the people they come from. They are authentic, true experiences – communicated with honesty and often a wry sense of humour. We are honoured to be able to bring these to print and they sum up, for us, why we love working for the organisations we do and making a difference in rural and remote Australia. We are both confident you will enjoy the read.

Proceeds from book sales go to both the RFDS and the CWA, so encourage others to buy or gift this book and share the joy. That would certainly make our efforts worthwhile.

And your feedback on Darn a Good Yarn is welcome through our Darn a Good Yarn Facebook page or through our website at **www.flyingdoctor.org.au/darn-good-yarn/**.

Lana Mitchell
Co-Editor, Royal Flying Doctor Service of Australia

Tanya Cameron OAM
Co-Editor, Country Women's Association of Australia

The Flying Doctor

– Jordan Verbeek

*Everything's so green in England,
Not out here in Oz.
Sun-baked, dirt-caked,
Dry and blistered,
Burnt brown through the hours.
Paled, sopping wet
And cold,
Stuck here for the maint'nance.*

*Three weeks in,
Two days out,
Working without weekend.
Half man posts,
And bags on roads,
Nothing used is wasted.
Flame grilled faces,
Flashing teeth,
Rare mates in these places.*

*Along up high, hello, goodbye,
The friendly skies are calling.*

Something is Not Quite Right...

– Alison Fox

I drank the juices of a dead frog for several days. My husband, Bruce, and I had taken a couple of weeks' leave and I returned to my job as Base Administrator for the RFDS in Meekatharra a few days ahead of him. On my first morning back, I boiled the kettle at home to make myself some coffee and I re-boiled it each morning until I noticed the water level was low. On about day four, I opened the lid to refill the kettle and found a dead frog floating around inside. It was white and bloated and had obviously been dead for some time.

And there I was, thinking the coffee tasted stale...

ONLY IN THE BUSH...

– *Kerri Betts*

As a child I was raised on a cattle station on the Queensland side of the Corner Country. Simpson desert. We were 100 mile plus from Tibooburra so relied on the Flying Doctor.

I always remember one particular day and that was when we were visiting family on the neighbouring property and at the time there was a couple living there, drilling bores. The wife had a bad accident with boiling water and the Flying Doctor was called. Everyone was with her, cutting her clothes off, etc.

The Flying Doctor was on the way and I was told to jump in the jeep and go to the dirt air strip to pick up the doctor. I would have been 8 or 9 years old but had driven jeeps for a while, living in the outback. This particular vehicle was an old Willys jeep. No doors, no brakes. Very rough.

So, when I could hear the plane coming I jumped in the jeep and took off for the air strip. It was a bit of a distance and the plane has landed by the time I got there. I couldn't stop the jeep so had to circle the plane and go down through the gears until it stopped.

The doctor was watching me and I kept telling him "it's okay I just don't have brakes".

So try to imagine what the poor doctor was thinking when he stepped from the plane.

No doors, no brakes and a child driving, propped up on pillows so I could see over the dash.

He hesitated and asked me was it safe to get in?

I said "Yes – Get in! I need to get you back there quick".

He didn't say much on his fast trip to the house. He did arrive safely however.

Congratulations to the Royal Flying Doctor Service and the Country Women's Association on over 9 decades of service to the country people! My husband and I have been married for fifty-seven years and lived in thirteen country towns and now live in Dalkeith Heights village Traralgon. I have been an active member of the CWA for fifty-seven years. Unfortunately poor health restricts what I can do now, but am still a member of CWA, Traralgon Branch.

Over the years the Royal Flying Doctor Service has been an invaluable help to me. I live with Parkinson's disease and multiple drug allergies. I spend a lot of time in hospitals and need respite in nursing homes. During these times I need to be taken to my neurologist in Melbourne by ambulance. I have lost count of the number of times the Royal Flying Doctor Service has looked after me. They excel in all that they do. Keep up the good work.

— Pam Landy

Quick Mix Apple Cake

```
2 cups self raising flour
1 tsp mixed spice
1 cup castor sugar
½ cup soft margarine
2 eggs
½ cup milk
1 small tin pie apple
Cinnamon
```

Beat all ingredients except the apple and cinnamon until smooth.

Put in greased slice tray, put apple on top with cinnamon sprinkled over.

Cook for 30 minutes at 180 degrees.

Never fails

(Recipe given to me by an elderly CWA member)

Ten Pound Pom

— **Michael Manning**

I'm an RFDS pilot in the RFDS South Eastern (NSW) company. Back in 2012 we were tasked to pick up a gentleman in his early eighties from Lake Cargelligo and then on to Wagga to pick up another patient and take them both to Sydney. While waiting for the ambulance at Wagga I started chatting to the elderly gentleman from Lake Cargelligo, who I sensed had an English accent. This is his story:

The day the school bell rang at 3:00pm on my 15th birthday I left school. I went to Birmingham, about three hours north of London and enrolled in a six-week course on how to be a farmer. I finished this course and worked on farms in the north while I waited to go into the army (as they had conscription at the time). Not long before I was due to go into the army they cancelled conscription, so I had to rethink my future.

At the time there was a scheme running which was similar to the 'Ten Pound Pom' ** but it was only for single males. I signed up to this scheme as "I had nothing better to do and it sounded like a bit of an adventure for a couple of years."

So I had free passage to Australia.

On arriving in Sydney I enrolled in another short course on how to be a farmer in Camden. Towards the end of this course a property owner rode in in search of a farm hand for his property in Lake Cargelligo. Having no idea where Lake Cargelligo was I put up my hand and said I'd go – so we both set off on horseback and rode from Camden to Lake Cargelligo.

During my seventh year of working on the property I entered and won a local lottery with the prize being 3,000 acres of undeveloped land in the area. With the money I had saved I planted a crop. As there were no fences I couldn't run any livestock. With the money I earned from my crop I put up some fences and over time I slowly developed the property.

During these years I met and married a local girl. My brother-in-law later bought the neighbouring property of 4,000 acres and from then on we ran it as one 7,000 acre property.

My wife and I ended up having seven healthy children. I've been back to England twice now, the first time it took me forty one years to go back and visit.

** Ten Pound Poms (or Ten Pound tourists) is a colloquial term used in Australia and New Zealand to describe British citizens who migrated to Australia and New Zealand after the Second World War. The Government of Australia initiated the Assisted Passage Migration Scheme in 1945. The migrants were called 'Ten Pound Poms' due to the payment of £10 in processing fees to migrate to Australia. The word Pom is derived from "pomegranate" – an Australian rhyming slang for "immigrant".

Stinky Cloves

– John Ascoli

In 1967 I was stationed in the Gulf at Wollogorang, Northern Territory. I lived at a one-man bush Police Station with my wife, Gillian, and sons Brenton 3 yrs, and Mark 2 yrs.

One morning Gillian found that my toddler Mark had drunk a small bottle of Oil of Cloves used for toothaches. Clove essential oil can be toxic to the nervous system and irritating to the skin and digestive mucous if taken in higher than recommended doses. Mark had taken way more than a standard dose.

Luckily the Flying Doctor from Mount Isa had just landed at the local airstrip and treated Mark with milk.

It worked – but Mark stunk for a week.

In those days we were a custodian for the local RFDS medical chest, that included morphine and all manner of other pharmaceuticals. Gillian, being a trained nurse, attended to emergency illnesses and injuries that occurred, and was the first responder for the Flying Doctor.

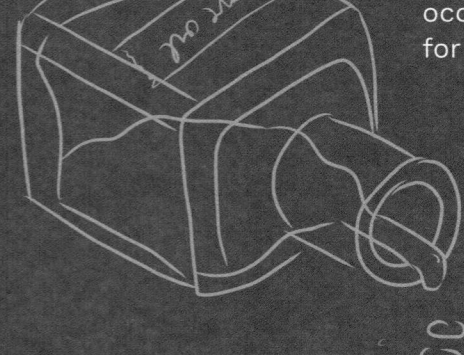

Breathe Easier

I was less than 12 hours old when I had my first RFDS flight from Mt Isa to Townsville.

I was very impatient to come into the world and had big feet so I kicked my way into the world at 26 weeks + 5 days.

I am now 7 years old and sometimes still need the friendly RFDS team to fly me out as I live in Cloncurry. Now I am older I sometimes get to 'fly' the plane!

I love the RFDS they are always so kind to me and help me breathe easier!

– Kayden Salsa

Old Pop

The Flying Doctor picked up Old Pop Aboriginal man from Mulgul station, in Western Australia many years ago.

It was a cold rainy night, and the old man had broken a leg when mustering cattle.

The RFDS pilot was only 19 years and the plane GPS had failed on their way back.

Old Pop guided the pilot to the Meekatharra airport, looking through the window every now and then, and directing from the air. They landed safely.

Many years later the RFDS pilot came back and told the story to the judge when we were fighting for our native title (which we won). He used the story to demonstrate that this is our country and we know it well.

— Connie Riley

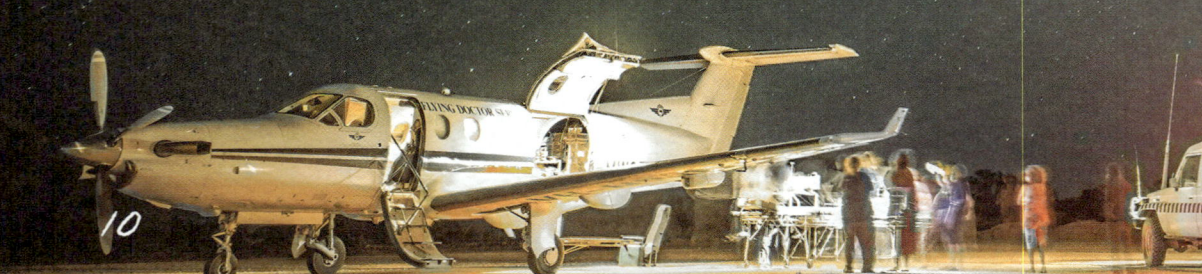

Memorable Flight

Just looking through some old log books and came across a memorable flight.

It was late March 2011 and the daytime temps were still topping 40 degrees on some days.

Two aircraft were tasked to a serious motor vehicle accident where it appeared that a kombi van full of tourists had rolled somewhere on the Tom Price to Wittenoom Road in remote Western Australia, with several people severely injured.

With no landing strips close by, it was decided that a road landing on site would be the best option, so one aircraft was tasked there and the other to Nanutarra. With the help of local police and some LandCruiser bull bars, all the offending road signs were flattened – allowing the RFDS aircraft to land safely on the highway itself.

Of the many injured, three young European tourists were picked up and transported back to Nanutarra, where our plane was waiting. One poor chap we had to look after had been thrown from the vehicle and landed on an ants nest, thus all his lacerations and other injuries were full of ants which need to be cleaned and sterilised.

Being of French nationality, his English was not great, though we managed to communicate well enough about the things that mattered. In 40 degree heat we prepped for flight.

Due to excessive hours on duty a mercy flight was declared and we departed for Jandakot around 7.30pm with one stop for fuel in Carnarvon. Some of those injured in the crash did not fare so well, with one girl dying and the other put into an induced coma to stabilise her.

By the time our flight reached the hotel in Perth we looked a sight for sore eyes with dust and blood streaked across our uniforms. Our patient and the other patients transported survived which makes it all worthwhile!

— Greg Phillips

Antique Aircraft Pilgrimage

— **Chris Gallagher**

To Dubbo we dared to venture.
A gaggle of antique planes joined us
For the start of a great adventure

From near and far they came that day
To commemorate the Flying Doctor
There were Tigers, 180s, Austers and Stinsons
But unfortunately there were no Proctors

A brace of Pipers and a CT4
A Birddog and Eagle no less
Aeronca, 140, and Leopard Moth
King Air of the RFDS

Leaving Dubbo on a cold clear morn
With the eyes of the world upon us
We headed to Moree over patchwork fields
Followed by Darren's big bus

The ladies of the Moree CWA
Displayed their culinary craft,
And the community came in their hundreds
To view the strange aircraft

A Civic reception followed
With drinks and nibbles provided
By Council and local businesses
Then a good night sleep to revive us

An early start to Roma
Tail winds and clear skies ahead
Security tight, spectators bag searched
At the Big Rig we were fed

Charleville's landscape was barren
A lost camera, a bit of a fright
BBQ at the RFDS base
And museum visit, a highlight

Then off to Longreach in strong winds
Landings in gusts rather tricky
In the shadow of the Jumbo jet
We were welcomed with cake and bickies

A sunset cruise on the Thomson
With supper and show was the call
Then a free day to rest before dinner
At the QANTAS founders hall

After repairs and rest we departed
On to Winton, in no time at all.
Where local school children were waiting
Viewing planes, they all had a ball

Bus trip to the Dinosaur Centre
To research geological past
Then back to the North Gregory Hotel
For a huge steak and chips repast

Bush flies were bad at Winton
Hat nets were the order of the day
But they could not stop the hassle
Of those caught in the cockpit on the way

Cloncurry was abuzz
With Flying Doctor things
We had no rest to catch our breath
Like roundabouts and swings

At Mary Kathleen mine museum
There were minerals abounding
Then out to Devoncourt to learn
Of history quite astounding

Back to town for more, more food
Meet the Governor and his wife
The John Flynn Place for welcome
Council dinner where speeches were rife

The re-enactment of the first flight
From Julia to the Curry
90 years after the event
Went by in such a hurry

*90 years of Flying Doc
is no small thing to do
thanks to all RFDS
Congrats to all of you*

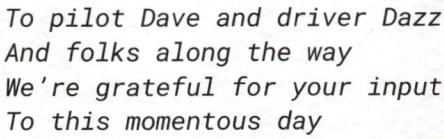

The final leg to Mt Isa
Then it was all but finished
Cake cutting at RFDS
Excitement not diminished

20 planes made it all the way
With just a few slight niggles
The company was fabulous
We all had lots of giggles

We enjoyed the company of Dave
Of Ian, Steve and Don
Of Vicki, Kevin, Pam and Pat
Of Woody, Mike, and John

Of Ben and Bill, Bruce and Bob
Of Kerry, Grant, and Wendy
Of Graeme, Keiran, Keith and Dan
Of Rhonda, Matt, and Cathy

Do not forget Ojars and Ross
Who rounded out the crews
Kale and Aden had in offer
More planes than they could choose

Our many thanks to David Theiss
Who came up with this view
Melissa, Kate and Lana
For making it come true

To pilot Dave and driver Dazz
And folks along the way
We're grateful for your input
To this momentous day

90 years of Flying Doc
Is no small thing to do
Thanks to all RFDS
Congrats to all of you

Them homeward bound from Isa
We went our separate ways
Those heading south had
strong headwinds
Which caused a few delays

All home safe and rested
We've memories galore
Would we do it all again?
The answers YES! I'm sure

All Dressed Up

— Michelle Campbell-Ward

Another Christmas was a-coming
The motionless air was hot and dry
The shorts and thongs and hats
were off
Out came the near new dress and tie

Almost festive party ready
Uncomfortably tailored and so smart
The time had come to celebrate
After a hard working week apart

The shrill ringing broke the silence
The GP said she'd phone by six
Should the blood test reveal anything
Even if only a tad amiss

At the hospital within the hour
The words were nervously spat out
"Leukaemia you have dear sir
And it is killing you, no doubt"

They said there was no time to waste
To 'big smoke' medics he must go
He replied in disbelief at once
Defiantly, a big fat "NO"

He had no means to get down there
And besides it was just a bruise
Too young, too well, too needed to
Accept that diagnosis. He'd refuse.

But the results were real
and frightening
A fatal bleed just hours away
Emergency transport had
been summoned
To get him there without delay

Thoughts arose of cancer,
chemo, death
And a vision of life uprooted
But what invoked the greatest fear?
The prospect of leaving here
smart suited!

Baby on board, no time to lose
Along dirt roads I cried and rushed
One long, fearful, panicked journey
To get his undies, boots and brush

Arriving at the dark air strip
I spied the hangar and the plane
My husband on a floodlit stretcher
My sheer relief I could not feign

The Aussie Flying Doctor
So trustworthy in their mission
Flew this dad and his country wear
To blessed safety and remission

Nana Peate's Curried Prawns, Circa 1974

– **Thomas Barratt**

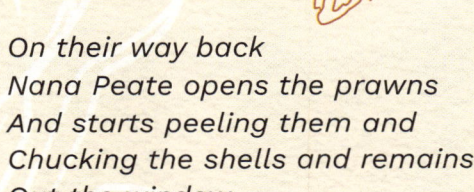

Be aware!
Nana Peate is cooking up
A special treat – curried prawns
The family is going to have
a feast.

Roll out the keg, wine, moselle,
Roll out the sausage rolls
And party pies

For desert – bread and butter
and strawberry conserve
And lamingtons

From the modest weatherboard
In a sleepy country town
Kurri Kurri – halfway between
Cessnock and Maitland –
a coal mining town

She makes her way to Newcastle
in Hillary's V8 Holden
Coming back into Hexham now.

They pick up the prawns and
continue on their way back
to Kurri Kurri.

On their way back
Nana Peate opens the prawns
And starts peeling them and
Chucking the shells and remains
Out the window.

"What are you doing?'
Aunt Hillary exclaims!
"Peeling them, no point
in leaving them to the last
minute,' Nana Peate said.

They arrived home, Nana Peate
opened the packet of prawns.
And says
'Stone the crows I've thrown the
prawns away and kept the shells.'

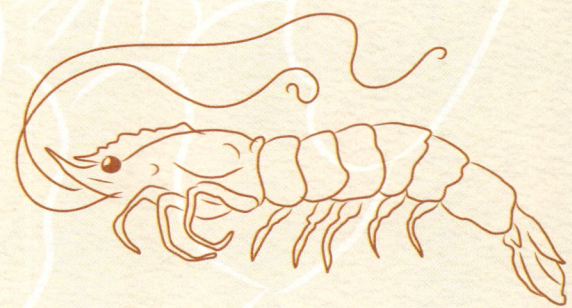

An Endless Sea of Stars

The night's magnificent silence is occasionally sullied by the drip of a drain, the soft hum of a pump motor, the wind through the trees its own music. The Milky Way floods the sky with a black stroke cutting down the middle, stars on either side burning brighter in defiance of the dark. Ten minutes for my eyes to adjust and the atmosphere explodes with stars covering the sky like dust, leaving fragments in my gaze.

A soft unidentifiable sound accompanies meteors of the Eta Aquarii shower lighting the sky with rushes of green, glowing blue and yellow. I know the colour is to do with the meteors' substance, but I don't care, with every burst of light the sound trembles as if it, like the stars shooting from the northern most aspect of the sky, has travelled from afar. It's only when I run out of breath I realise the sound is mine, my mouth making oh, oh, oh puffs of warm breath.

The trees look like shadows against the sky, paper cut-outs moving with the wind, dancing as if each fallen star causes the movement. Pressing my fingers against the sky, I'm certain I can feel the passing of each meteor, tracing shapes in the Milky Way. My black Labrador, Hugo is curled up beside me, snuggled tight on an old cane sun lounge, wrapped in a doona, snoring heavily. The mosquitoes are annoying, and snacks other than carrots would've been a good idea.

As eyes adjust, my fingers pick out fresh shapes in the stars, my skills of join the dots improving, soon I'll be a Mr. Squiggle pro.

— *Alex Dunn*

Tracing the shape of Australia from eras before, when the west was lost to a whisper and the east coast the straight line of a cartographer's gleeful guess at the void. There is nothing of where I am now, the coastal living of Lennox Head and my Seven Mile beach missing, invisible. I sketch a whale flowing around the shape of Tasmania, images from Moby Dick, of the dangers of an intoxicating obsession. I know more of Herman Melville now, 'Without imagination no man can follow another'. My imagination is free, at rest, following every exploding comet, having discovered a new world, a treasure just for me and the black dog at my side. I can dream here, I am someone else, somewhere else.

The images floating from the stars are too eager for the sky to contain, sprinting across the heavens, limitless with surprise, a miracle. The left of the sky is blocked by trees and rather than put up with it, I feel the best and clearest view would be from the beach.

Leaving the empty house behind, Hugo and I traipse across driveways lit with sensor lights, a darkened field occupied by an angry, lonely, tick-infested stallion who grudgingly accepts a proffered carrot, across roads and down streets. The sun is two hours from rising, the darkness affecting us only with the calm it brings, the solitude.

We make our way down the stairs cut into the Pat Morton lookout, the sound of waves roiling, the rhythm crashing against the rocky shore. Ten minutes and we're running on the sand, I'm kicking off sneakers and socks like a child, bare feet soaking up the cold of the sand with relish, shouting with excitement when I see the pounding currents swirling with blue lights.

Bioluminescence.

The water rolls with colour, shimmering lights marking a path as if leading me in, reflecting the shooting stars above.

Race you! Hugo shouts, barking a laugh, jumping on glowing patches as if he can catch them. Our feet ignite the sand in blue fire as we run, like a match to a fuse.

It's almost too much; the beauty, the quiet, the peace. The wavy line of the horizon speckled with glowing dust.

The water is freezing but I run in anyway, jumping glowing waves to dive into the illuminated depths. I surface, spitting salty blue stars and laughing as Hugo tries to use me as a flotation device. The shining water runs down my naked body, freckles painted bright blue, hair dripping starshine.

I lie as still as possible in the rough currents, a small rip somewhere to the left of us, watching the green stars shoot overhead and the carpet of blue phosphorescence settling around us. Hugo's still trying to catch the glow, duck-diving, coming up snorting blue. I can't stop laughing; stomach cramping, tear leaking, rolling laughs which echo from the sand dunes.

I long to stay here forever. I'm shivering, my fingers and toes numb but I want to hold tight to the warmth within me. I'm possessive of the exquisite sensation of floating in an endless sky, stars running down my arms as I lift them from the water, as colours shoot above, two streaks per minute. I try to cup the radiant water in my hands, thinking to carry some home, to keep it with me, yet I know I can't, because it's not mine. I wish I could show this to the world, bring them here. Maybe it's here all the time but I just never thought to come at night, at the right time.

Hugo's ashore, rolling in the sand, his footprints edged with blue.

My skin glimmering with light, I leave the water's tug, shoving my jumper and jeans over cold sticky skin, sand clinging and chaffing.

Whatever damage the hardship of a changing world has done, it hasn't taken the last of me, I'm still here, with a muddy dog by my side. The flame may be banked, but I smile, realising there's life, light, in a place I believed desolate.

FLASH FLOOD AND NO PHONE!

– Lorne Henry

I did experience the work of the Flying Doctor in the far south-west of Queensland in the late 50s (1957-8) and thought them wonderful. The shearers' cook had cut his leg with an axe and needed help badly but there had been a rare flash flood and we could not get out. The telephone wires had been blown down and the generator had broken down, needing another part.

A jackaroo went by horse (60 miles) to get the part and fixed the telephone wire as he went, allowing us to get through to the Flying Doctor. As there'd been just another sprinkling of rain, the runway was like ice (slippery) so he couldn't land, but medication and instructions were dropped wrapped in rubber blanketing. Two women on the station played doctor. I remember standing on a tank stand watching the plane circling overhead, with everyone waving madly.

The only way the jackaroo had of getting over the roaring creek was to have a rope tied around him as the horse swam through. He then tied that same rope to a tree (a coolabah of course) and that allowed him to get back after picking up the part from Quilpie.

I must say that we all had a wonderful time without the electricity; playing cards every night by lamp light. The old flat irons came out for the older lady of the house to iron the sheets! Why she felt she had to that is a bit beyond me! Times have certainly changed.

Without question, without the phone line and the Flying Doctor the chef would have been in quite a mess. Here's to the Royal Flying Doctor Service!!

Tribute to Winifried Violet Crisp

— Dianne Smith,
Secretary
Swansea Branch
of CWA Tasmania

This is a story about my Grandmother, Mrs. Winifred Violet Crisp and her time in CWA, as transcribed by my Aunt, Mrs. Margaret Crisp.

Mrs. Winifred Crisp was born in England in 1898 and spent her childhood in Colchester, Essex in South East England. After leaving school during the First World War, she became a volunteer nurse, nursing wounded servicemen in Cambridge near Colchester.

Mr. George Ellis Crisp had been posted to an Officers Training School in Cambridge after being gassed in France and it was here he met the then Winifred Watson. They married in June 1919 after the war and returned to Tasmania in January 1920 and settled on the family property of 'Lewis Hill', east of Avoca, on the St. Paul's River.

For a young and pregnant war bride from the other side of the world, who had never lived outside a city and never learnt to cook, this was a very daunting and lonely time as 'Lewis Hill' was isolated and without electricity until 1940. She became an extremely competent mother, housewife, cook, seamstress (making many of the clothes for her 5 children – the eldest of whom was my Mother), gardener and also an avid reader.

The family moved from the cottage to the large homestead on the property in 1940, which entailed taking over and managing the small local telephone exchange and Post Office until 1954, when these services were moved to the small town of Royal George.

She was the organist at St. Paul's Church in Royal George for many years and a great community worker at church fairs, etc.; but most of all for the Country Women's Association in Tasmania. She was the founding member and President of the Avoca Branch, (later the Avoca/Royal George Branch), when it was formed in 1944. Membership soon grew from the original 11 to 49 members and much of the work was for the war effort – knitting, packing food parcels for servicemen, raising money for the Red Cross, Comforts Fund and Prisoner of War Fund.

Violet held office in the Avoca Branch for many years, in several capacities. She was Eastern Group President for 3 terms, then Tasmanian State President for 3 years (1956-1959) and a term of 3 years as National President. She was also a delegate at the Associated Country Women of the World (ACWW) Conference in Columbo (now Sri Lanka) and was then appointed Co-ordinating Committee Chairperson for the following World Conference in Melbourne in 1962.

My grandmother was made a Life Member of CWA in Tasmania in 1961, within the Eastern Group, (now defunct) the Winifred Crisp Trophy was awarded annually for preserves, the winning entry going on to represent the Eastern Group in the State Exhibition. She will probably be best remembered for the Winifred Crisp Book Of Honour awarded to the Branch presenting the best Annual report in the State and is still awarded to this day. The founding of this award reflected the great importance Mrs. Crisp placed on this aspect of CWA and she ran many Leadership Schools throughout the state, to encourage members to hold office and so contribute with confidence and efficiency to the well-being of CWA, the association she loved so much and served so well.

Mrs. Crisp, my "Nanna", who passed away in 1974, was the inspiration for me to become a member of the CWA in Tas. Inc.

Barley Broth

My mother would have started making this back in 1932 and my grandmother long before that. And I'm sure my grandmother's mother made it before then. It's a great first solids for the baby — you can strain it, mash it, or, nowadays, just put it in the food processor. For adults, you can add an onion to it, but you wouldn't want to give the babies onion. I know the babies these days have all the canned food but this is so easy, so much healthier and a lot cheaper. My four children never had cans and neither do my six grandchildren, not when I can make them Barley Broth.

4 lamb shanks
3 litres water
2 teaspoons salt
3 carrots, chopped
2 sticks celery, chopped
1 potato, chopped
1 parsnip, chopped
1½ cups pearl barley
Chopped parsley, to serve

Trim excess fat off meat then place with water and salt in a large saucepan. Bring slowly to the boil and simmer for 1½ hours. Remove from stove and add chopped vegetables and pearl barley. Simmer for 1½ hours.

Remove meat from bones and add to the soup. Reheat.

For infants, press through a sieve. For adults, sprinkle with chopped parsley and serve with a crusty roll. Can be frozen successfully.

— Noela Macleod,
Essendon CWA

Just Too Long

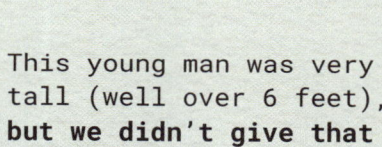

I am a recently retired Registered Nurse. For most of my working life I worked in rural and remote areas of South Australia.

I remember an incident in the early 80s when I was on duty at the Ceduna Hospital on the far west coast of South Australia.

We received notification that a young farmer had had an accident and the tractor had run over him. On arrival it was clear that he was in a bad way and the x-ray confirmed a fractured femur, so we stabilised the fracture with a Hare traction splint.

This young man was very tall (well over 6 feet), **but we didn't give that a thought.**

We called the RFDS and the plane came to collect him. The ambulance took him out to the airstrip but they couldn't load him on because he wouldn't fit in the plane. His height plus the extra length of the splint just didn't go. So they had to bring him back to hospital and send for another longer plane.

From then on we had to provide the RFDS measurements of all patient transfers. The patient made a full recovery and I often see him on trips back to the coast.

– Meredith McInnis

My Life Line

— Jennifer Hetherington

After living for the past 40 years in many parts of isolated Australia and having to call on the RFDS several times I have only just taken the time to make my ongoing monthly donation to them — a donation that I am more than happy to make as I could not put a price on my family's lives.

My story begins with the first time I ever needed to call on the RFDS in 2002, after **my husband decided to cut off his thumb with a bandsaw on a cattle property 130 kilometres from Winton.** The Flying Doctor called the Queensland Ambulance Service to assist us with transportation from the property to the Winton Airstrip, where my husband was flown to Townsville for emergency surgery. Yes, his thumb was thankfully saved.

My second time needing these angels was when **my father was critically ill with heart failure and needed to be flown to heart specialists in Brisbane.** The Flying Doctor took delivery of him from the Intensive Care Unit in the Mount Isa Hospital and safely handed him over to the specialists in Brisbane. I caught a domestic flight to Brisbane with my mother and stayed with him for the two weeks' duration he was there.

On discharge day, when I returned to the station we lived on in the Gulf of Carpentaria, I set down my bags and proceeded towards the school room to greet my children and their governess. My four year old was so eager to show me her painting that was drying on the ground that she pulled me by the hands and **then picked up the picture that unbeknown to us had a snake under it. My four year old then took the brunt of the snake bite — which put all of us into hysteria.** A call to the RFDS was made. Within three hours we were retrieved and set down in the intensive care unit of the Mount Isa Hospital. **I had not even had time to unpack my bag from my Dad's visit — just picked it up and walked out the door heading straight for the airstrip in Burketown.** After a day in intensive care we were discharged with no concerns.

> *"My four year old was so eager to show me her painting that was drying on the ground that she pulled me by the hands and then picked up the picture that unbeknown to us had a snake under it."*

My fourth encounter with the RFDS was 7 weeks after the birth of my fourth daughter. We had been out socializing in Burketown for the night and on our return to the station **she was crying uncontrollably, after undressing her (as we thought she may have been bitten by something) we were met with a large dark mass protruding from her stomach.**

My husband was instructed to try to push the intestines of his 7 week-old baby back in the opening and to keep applying pressure until the RFDS arrived. This was the longest wait we had ever gone through – though admittedly it probably wasn't that long. We were retrieved and transported to the Mount Isa Hospital where a paediatric surgeon was sent by the RFDS from Townsville to transport us from Mount Isa to Townsville. This all went without a hitch and after my baby had abdominal surgery the next day we were on our way home.

Our fifth encounter with the Flying Doctor came 18 months later when the abdominal surgery on my infant become undone. By then we were living remotely in the Northern Territory and lucky for us the nearby Indigenous settlement had a permanent nurse who took us in and took control. Next thing we were transported (once again) by the RFDS to Alice Springs hospital for new surgery to remedy the problem.

Over the years of working on cattle properties we have had to call on the RFDS for many things from horse accidents, to car accidents, to just sickly children. How do you put a price on that type of care? It is priceless.

We owe many lives to the wonderful doctors and nurses that make up the RFDS and we will forever give our thanks.

The Hetherington Family.

– Robyn Muller

Bogged in Pentland!

The airstrip in Pentland, Queensland in 1964 was not of international standards by any means! It was rough, it was short and it ran from the sawmill through the middle of the local race course and pulled up just short of Betts Creek.

On the rare occasion that a plane actually landed in Pentland it was a big deal, so when the Flying Doctor visited on his two monthly clinics it was a huge occasion!

The landing strip was maintained by locals and dragged with mesh gates to keep it free of rocks and shrubs. When it rained the track became quite boggy and had to be physically inspected before any aircraft could land. The message to the pilot would be relayed via wireless to inform of suitability to land.

The wet season in Pentland in 1964 had been exceptional with a more than average rainfall, much to the delight of the local graziers who were fattening their cattle for sale to the recently re-opened Cape River Meatworks.

The runway, positioned just 800 yards (yes, it was yards in those days) from town was an easy pick up by the rostered hack to collect the doctor and take him to the clinic (which was under the double story residence and adjoining shop of Len and Betty Pilcher in the Main Street).

And the strip was even closer to the local Police Station, a mere 400 yards yonder. The local copper in Pentland at the time, Sergeant Maurie Hanson, was an affable and popular chap who had formed a firm friendship with the infamous RFDS Dr. Tim O'Leary who was based in Charters Towers.

Photographs by Mervin Pilcher

On this occasion, Dr. O'Leary had just finished a western clinic and landed in Pentland for the scheduled clinic and to have a cuppa with his mate Maurie. The three engine Drover aircraft made a perfect landing but lost speed and tipped on its nose before settling belly deep in the mud! And it stayed that way for 2 weeks! So much for track inspections and wireless communication!

Dr O'Leary and the pilot retreated to Charters Towers via the eastbound train 'The 19 DOWN'.

In the meantime locals and self-appointed salvage experts managed to dig and pull the plane out of the bog using man power, pullies and sleeper logs from the saw mill. Budding photographer, historian and inventor, Mervin Pilcher, was on hand to take photographs of the furore!

Dr O'Leary and the pilot returned 2 weeks later on the westbound train 'The 44 UP' to salvage the plane – which incidentally started first go and took off without further incident!

Many versions and interpretations from eye witnesses have faded or been rehashed. Some doubt if it really was Dr. Tim O'Leary at the helm at the time. It appears that 'ol Doc O'Leary was a brilliant and caring doctor, a sociable character, a jockey, a bushie and didn't mind a drop of the amber fluid – which explains why he had made such a memorable impact on our locals that even 50 years later he is spoken of in high esteem. But not one to get in the way of a darn good yarn I choose to stick to this version, and whether this is a truest version or not the photographs tell the tale precisely!

I Remember the Fires at Take-Off

- Vicki

My first trip on an RFDS plane was 57 years ago at the age of 3.

We lived on a cattle station in the NT and I had had a fall causing a very nasty large scalp laceration.

My Dad had to light fires along the edge of the airstrip as the evacuation happened late in the evening.

I can still vividly remember when we were taking off seeing the glow of the little fires from the air.

I travelled on my own (no escort) as the flight nurse was well known to all the station families, so no hesitation to send me off on my lonesome.

Apparently she stayed with me at the hospital as I went into theatre with a general anaesthetic to be sutured up.

I have had many more flights as an adult but now they are work related.

Fantastic work the RFDS do all over the country.

Chicken Pie

- 1 Tbls oil
- 1 small onion, chopped
- 1 small potato, grated
- 1 Tbls cornflour
- 250 g cooked chicken
- 600 mL chicken stock
- 130g can mushrooms in butter sauce
- A little lemon juice
- Salt and pepper to taste
- 1 egg, beaten
- 2 Tbls cream
- 2 sheets puff pastry

Preheat oven to 210 °C.

Heat oil and cook onion and potato. Add cornflour and cook for a few more minutes. Remove from heat and add chicken stock. Return to heat and stir until mixture thickens.

Add chicken, mushrooms, lemon juice and salt and pepper. Mix egg with cream, then add to chicken mixture.

Line a deep 20cm pie dish with one sheet of puff pastry. Fill with mixture. Wet pastry edges and cover with remaining pastry sheet. Trim and seal edges. Glaze top with a little milk. Make a slit in the top of pastry to allow steam to escape.

Bake for 30 minutes, until pastry is crisp and golden. It's also nice cold.

– Licia Lawford, Frankston CWA

I was bitten by a king brown snake while living on a remote cattle station 450km out of Tennant Creek. I was 3 years old at the time.

I'm now 27 and living life to the fullest in the big smoke. I owe my life and more to the RFDS as there is no way I would have survived the long drive to town that night.

Here is my my Dad's encounter of that late Sunday night we'll never forget:

— Alexandra Sheehy

NOT TOO LATE

— Michael Sheehy

I worked in the bush for a few years.
Been run over by a cow or two.
I've seen the inside of the Flying Doctor plane
on more than one occasion.
I was lucky when some I know weren't.
Sometimes it doesn't matter when the
plane arrives.
Sometimes it's just too late.

I'm still here.

My three year old daughter was bitten
by a king brown snake
one Sunday night in the bush.
It was late at night.
A big bush BBQ.
A going-away party.

It was our time to leave the bush.
I had a family to school.
Bush kids have the run of the place.
Always in motion, squealing.
Wild and free.
Falling over boundaries.
Bouncing right back up.

It's late at night.
Kids love a party.
A special time.
Maybe the last time.
Laughter and squeals fill the air.

A scream cuts the night.
A solitary sound.
Fair dinkum sound.
Unmistakable.
It is the quiet kid.
She rarely spoke.
She never yelled.
Everyone is drunk.
Parents now sober.
A bright fluorescent light.
No mistaking a snake bite.

Capable hands come to the fore.
Bandages appear.
Compression is the key.
Calm demeanours.
You cannot panic.
No one can.
Soothing words.
A child's wide eyed fear.
A parents terror.
Mad dash to the phone.

It's late.
It's Sunday.
You know you're drunk.
But you're not.
You can't be.
"Hello, we need a plane"
"Did you see the snake?"
"You know it's late?"
"Have you been drinking?"
"Mate I know it's late"
"My daughter is just a baby"
"I have been in the bush a long time"
"I know I sound rough"
"It's late"
"It is a snake bite"
"A big snake, most likely a brown"
"A king brown"
"I need a plane"

They came.
We were prepared.
We had done this before.
Car headlights at either end.
Milk tins each side of the strip.
Hundred paces apart.
Sand, kerosene and dry grass.
They would burn for hours.

They had done this before.
Tennant Creek was the nearest hospital.
Near on 450 km by car.
Only angels could get there in time.
There was more than one angel on board.
Sure hands.
Steely eyes.
It's late.
Not too late.
The child is small.
Still.
Her colour grey.
The child is breathing.
Sharp and short.
No time to waste.
We have to go.

Not all could fit inside.
There were six of us.
Mother, a boy on the breast.
The door closes.
Is that it.
No time to say goodbye.
A final goodbye.
Dad and two big sisters left on the strip.

The sisters are just babies.
All are numb.
Engines roar at take off.

Silence.
A faint blinking light disappears
into the milky way.
The lights on the strip go out.
Darkness blankets the night.

Now morning.
You stare for an eternity.
The house seems empty.
Silent.

She was always the quiet one.
You try to comfort the sisters.
There are no words.
The void cannot be filled.
You just hold each other tight
and pray.
Make promises.

Today my three year old
is twenty seven.
We talk most days.
As close as you can be.
One of the lucky ones.
We are the lucky ones.

It wasn't too late.

Indebted

– Lee-Anne Waters

On the 27th of April 2010 I had a gall operation in Bundaberg, Queensland.

Before being flown out I almost died twice due to major complications, one of which was fluid leaking into my body.

I needed these "Angels of the Sky" to fly me to Royal Brisbane Hospital. The 45 minute flight was the most memorable moment of my 5 week stay in 2 hospitals.

Up in the sky I was pain free for the first time due to the plane being pressurized and me being on morphine.

The doctor on board and my pilot were truly awesome.

I owe my life to this service being available for those that live in the bush and on the coast.

Thank you again so very much. I am indebted to you and always support your wonderful service. My mum also has been a user of this wonderful service, nearly 15 years ago.

BUDGIE EXPLOSION

In 1988 the budgies bred up after big rains. These photos were taken at Maralinga airport, Australian Protective Service base, at hospital and surrounding buildings, in South Australia.

Not a Matter of if, But a Matter of When

— Jodie Grant

When we first moved to the outback a very wise neighbour told me that when you stay out bush long enough, at some point every member of your family will need the Flying Doctor.

She said it is not a matter of if, but a matter of when.

And those words were absolutely true.

Myself, my husband and a number of our staff have all used the Flying Doctor service. And my children have benefitted from the RFDS medical chests for minor ailments that didn't require flying out.

The RFDS is a service we will always give money to — and respect in the highest regard.

"Doc" Sims

– *Gloria Willis*

When my father, Stephen Sims, was a young teenager in 1932, he and his family lived on a small farm close to the Archerfield Aerodrome (Brisbane Qld). My grandfather, George Sims, was an English immigrant who bought this land in approximately 1913. He was a farmer but in the late 1920s he had a carting accident and had to have his right arm amputated from above the elbow. This meant he had to seek alternate employment and leave the farming work to his family. He luckily found employment at the newly opened Archerfield Aerodrome as a night watchman. He had many stories to tell of "near misses" and of early flying characters.

One day he came home from work and asked my father if he (Stephen) would like to be in a film. He explained that he had met some people at his work who intended to make a documentary about the Royal Flying Doctor Service, which would be shown later on the newsreel at the Picture Theatres. They had asked George if he knew of a boy who would be willing to do this and earn "a few bob". The role Stephen would be asked to play was that of a young person who was to fall off his horse in front of the camera, and then lay still on the ground until the RFDS aircraft came to pick him up and take him off to hospital. My father was quite happy to do this as he had heard of Reverend John Flynn and the work he was doing in Western Queensland and occasionally saw the Flying Doctor planes at the Archerfield Aerodrome.

So the day came, the camera crew were assembled at a certain point and all my father had to do was to gallop along on his pony and when he was in front of the camera, he just had to fall off. Simple!

So he galloped along and as he approached the camera everyone started shouting "fall off", "fall off". He could not do it, it was going to hurt too much.

> "Stephen became a licensed aircraft maintenance engineer and gained his pilot's licence in 1937. From his association with the RFDS he was given the nickname of 'Doc.'"

He was successful however on the second attempt, fell off right in front of the camera and there he lay waiting to be picked up by the RFDS. This plane had arrived earlier and with the camera rolling taxied across the airstrip to attend to its "patient". The doctor and his assistant jumped out of the plane, examined him, then put him on a stretcher, and with help carried him to the waiting aircraft. It then took off for a circle around the aerodrome.

He couldn't remember if he received any payment for his performance and did not get a chance to go and see it at the Picture Theatre – but that became his claim to fame.

Stephen became a licensed aircraft maintenance engineer and gained his pilot's licence in 1937. From his association with the RFDS he was given the nickname of "Doc". In 1950 he was working for QANTAS when they moved their business from Archerfield to Eagle Farm.

He decided to leave Archerfield aerodrome and took up farming but gave that up when my mother passed away in 1959. He then went back to repairing aircraft through Western/Northern Queensland and met up with many RFDS pilots of his day and heard of their wonderful stories of saving lives of the station people.

He was known by everyone as "Doc" Sims. He always supported the Service when he could.

After he retired he enjoyed meeting up with friends associated with light aircraft and one such person was a doctor who had in his younger days worked with the RFDS. At my father's funeral in 1998 I met the wife of this doctor and she showed me a photo of their newly purchased light aircraft. They acquired its registration number of VH-DOC in honour of my father and his dedication to years of working with light aircraft.

In his words he would have been "tickled pink" to know about this honour and also to have his story told.

In the mid to late 1970s, my family lived at Bindara House on Tandou Station. Here is one memorable incident I wanted to share.

HELP, I'VE KILLED MICHAEL!

"Help, I've killed Michael",
I screamed out to Mum.
Our tree climbing race,
Had gone horribly wrong.

His branch had broken,
And with a reverse double pike,
He had fallen and landed,
Head first on a spike.

Mum rushed from the chook house,
Dropping the eggs,
As she saw blood pouring down,
From his head to his legs.

Grabbing the Traeger radio,
With shaking hands and a cry,
Mum put out a call,
To the Doc in the sky.

Explaining the symptoms
Mum said with a groan,
"There's a great flap of skin,
"And I can see bone".

I thought - she'll become,
Patient number two,
And if she passes out,
What the heck will I do?

Calmly a voice said,
"No need for the plane,
"It's good there is blood,
"And that it's not brain."

"Just cut off the skin,
"And clean up a bit,
"All the stuff that you need's
"In the medicine kit."

It was the first time we called them,
But it wasn't the last,
As more misadventures,
And accidents passed.

There aren't enough words,
To really express,
Our respect and our thanks
To Broken Hill RFDS.

— Julie Crisp (née Davidson)

– Dianne Bailey

Family Cook at 8 Years

Back in the days when the Flying Doctor out of Port Augusta was still a volunteer post, my late mother Nesta Bailey, had to take a flight to bring in a sick Aboriginal child.

She was not a nurse, just a volunteer with the RFDS Auxiliary, but was always willing to help.

As a result of this mercy mission, I, at the age of 8 years old, got to cook my first meal for Dad and my two younger siblings. The meal turned out OK (thankfully) – and the Aboriginal baby was soon well enough to go back to its mother.

Reflections

Part of my job as RFDS Meekatharra Base Administrator entailed entering data into the computer. Any time an RFDS doctor was consulted remotely, whether by phone or radio, they had to complete a "Remote Consultation Form" detailing the call. It was important to keep these records but I know administrators at other bases often hated this more tedious aspect of our work.

For me, though, it was interesting to read about the reasons why patients or their carers called for medical advice, and what advice the doctors gave them. Some calls resulted in the aircraft being called out but often the doctor came up with other solutions to the patients' problems, such as accessing medication from a medical chest if they had one, or if it wasn't serious, encouraging them to see their GP or community nurse at the next opportunity.

Some of the reasons why our doctors were contacted, I saw, included suspected heart attacks, problem pregnancies, broken limbs and any number of assorted physical ailments. There were calls after workplace accidents, car accidents and injuries from fights. Sadly there were sometimes calls for psychological help as well.

Our doctors were called about dog bites, snake bites, spider bites and insect bites. I recall reading about a plane that was called out for a suspected sea-snake bite as well as a crocodile bite in northern WA, and on one occasion, a box jellyfish sting. One man was flown to hospital after being gored by a bull and another who'd been attacked by a shark. I was surprised to learn, however, that the animals which caused the most injuries were horses, whether from falls or kicks or being dragged along with one foot in the stirrup after coming out of the saddle.

As I worked through the many documents, I came to appreciate just how important it must be for people living in remote areas to be able to call the RFDS for medical help or advice, whatever the problem. Without the Service, a lot of people would be in trouble...

– Alison Fox

Nullabor Challenge

— Diane Janseen

In the year 2000 I went out on the Nullabor to the Road House at Madura.

We had to help people out that had run into trouble.

A truckie had pulled off the road in a bad way. He had climbed into the back and his wife was driving.

We had a struggle getting him out of the back of the truck.

We called the Flying Doctor and as it was getting dark we had to go and light the drums on our makeshift runway so that the plane could safely land in the dark.

The RFDS, risking their lives, came to the rescue and saved this man's life.

This is just one of the million stories of the wonderful Flying Doctor.

– Mrs Pat Punch, Chairman of the Show Catering Committee of the CWA Victoria

We've been associated with the Royal Melbourne Show since 1935 but we built the annex back in 1954. We bake the scones today in the same green enamel Federal Gas Oven that was used back then. Goodman Fielder donates fourteen 25kg bags of flour each year and we use every one. We probably make around 100 dozen scones a day. We have 24 ladies come down to help out for the whole 11 days and we all stay at the CWA club. We leave in a bus about 5.30 each morning and then head back in the bus at the end of the day. It's like a family: there is great camaraderie between us all. We love sitting down for dinner and having a chat about the day and all the funny things that have happened. There are also about 20 to 25 helpers who meet us at the Show to help out for a day. Yes, it is a big commitment because we also have to clean the place for two days before we open and then clean up for a day after. But we love it, and we raise a lot of money.

Show Scones

8 cups self-raising flour
1 tsp salt
500mL cream
750-800mL milk
Melted butter

Preheat oven to 250°C and grease baking trays.

Add the cream to the sifted flour and salt and slowly add enough to mix to a soft dough. Roll out and cut into a decent size. Bake 10 to 15 minutes.

When cooked, brush tops and bottoms with melted butter. It removes any flour and helps to keep them nice and soft.

Technical Problem

– *Alison Fox*

Working from our RFDS base at Meekatharra could be lonely at times, especially if our aircraft was called out to fly on a patient retrieval or rescue. On those occasions, the doctor, nurse and pilot could all be out for the day and sometimes the night as well. I'd often be alone in the office with not another soul for company. At least, not another human soul…

The airport was six kilometres out of Meeka, itself a small town with limited services, so if I had a problem – such as office machinery breaking down – it could be difficult to get help.

One morning, I tried to run off some photocopies but I noticed the dreaded 'paper jam' light flashing on the machine. I opened the relevant panels but could find no paper stuck anywhere. There being no photocopier technicians for several hundred kilometres around, I called our technical team in Perth.

"What's up, Alison?"

"The photocopier's indicating a paper jam but I can't see paper stuck in the usual places."

"Have you tried all the check panels?"

"Yes, but I can't see anything. I really don't know what's going on."

The ever-patient technician led me through a number of steps to get into the delicate workings of the machine and after a while, I said, "I've found what's wrong! You'll never guess."

"You're right, I'll never guess."

"It's an egg!

"An egg? What sort of egg?"

"Well, it…"

And before I could finish, a small lizard dashed out from under the machine and took off down the corridor to the nurses' room, tail in the air.

"It was a lizard! She's laid eggs inside the machine and one of them somehow broke. There are bits of eggshell in the feed roller."

"I've had some strange problems to deal with but a lizard laying eggs in the photocopier hasn't been one of them till now…"

Tribute to Nancy Bird (Walton)

Having known fellow woman pilot, Nancy Bird (Walton) since 1962, her emphasis was always on the use of aviation for medical use.

Nancy started transporting nurses and medical supplies to remote areas back in 1935 when she bought her own small plane and put it to good use.

Nancy Bird was the youngest female commercial pilot in the British Empire at age 19…what a success story she was!

She was never short of a word of encouragement and was working as a guest speaker close to her ending years. I was her driver for the last 6 active years of her demanding speaking career, when she inspired her audiences with stories of the Royal Flying Doctor Service, Air Ambulance and my own passion for the Helicopter Rescue Services.

It was such a surprise to me when driving south from Darwin that I found a section of the highway designated to the Royal Flying Doctor Service aircraft (see the threshold markers on the highway) and there were parking bays for the road ambulances, carrying patients who needed the aviation services.

I am so proud of how Australia has used aviation for medical services and did my best promoting helicopter rescue services and public-use helipads back in 1976, prior to the first service being established, "The Wales Helicopter Service" based at LongReef, flown by Allan Edwards in the 1970s.

I was instrumental in establishing the first public-use helipad in Sydney, 1983.

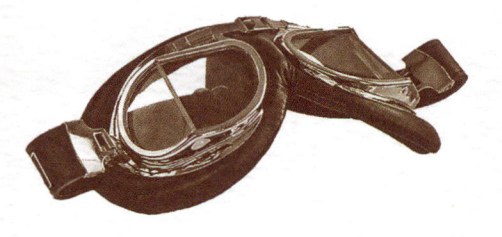

— Rosemary Arnold

End of an Era

1960s School of The Air over radio

– **Sally Henery**

I wrote this poem in late 2002 when the Port Augusta School of the Air switched off their HF Radio channels and switched over to the Internet to deliver school lessons to the students scattered across outback South Australia.

I came to the Flinders Ranges from Adelaide at age 17 to work as a Governess on Gum Creek Station and then Holowiliena Station, supervising School of the Air lessons and curriculum to the school-aged children on the stations, followed by several stints governessing children of three families living in Blinman in the centre of the beautiful Flinders Ranges.

I met my future husband in Blinman and we married and lived at Alpana and had two children of our own who in turn became School of the Air students. They were both involved in the Internet lessons trial in 2002 and this trial was so successful that the whole school changed to Internet in 2003.

The RFDS and School of the Air were intrinsically linked by the umbilical cord of the HF Radio coax cables and there was a palpable sense of nostalgia and sentiment at the big change from the traditional HF Radio delivery of lessons to the then very new and slightly intimidating world wide web and satellite Internet technology.

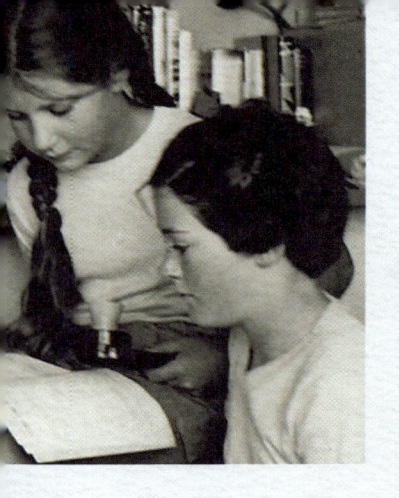

The airways are silent over outback SA
But close your eyes tightly; you may hear, far away
A chorus of voices, some small and some strong
Soft whispering echoes of The School of Air song.

Tourists and friends would listen and smile
When they chose to tune in and feel a part, for a while
Of Fundays and laughter, songs, jokes and views
Forty-five years of lessons, assemblies and news.

The spirit and pride of each isolated child
With dusty bare feet and a warm honest smile
You can feel in your soul, in the heart of this land,
When you stand still a moment, squeeze some
dirt in your hand.

The Flying Doctor radios, a staple of life
For people on stations or travellers in strife
Or Distance Ed students attending their classes
Once filled outback airways with crackly voices.

Old aerial wires sag, black coax hangs stiff
As a breeze whistles past a new satellite dish
Mounted high on the roof, a high-tech round face
Brings the world to the bush, beaming voices
through space.

High Frequency waves are now no longer used
As the Internet carries students' learning and news
Think back on the past, look next to the future
Understand the nostalgia in the final "Cheers Over".

Now the airways are silent over outback SA
But close your eyes tightly, you may hear, far away
A chorus of voices, some small and some strong
Soft whispering echoes of The School of Air song.

Current School of the Air Student, Henry

King Island Resident for 50 Years

– Cynthia Stellmaker

Living on King Island, emergencies were responded to by the Royal Flying Doctor Service based at Essendon airport in Melbourne.

Our first experience was on the first Saturday in November 1990.

My late husband was playing a good game of tennis until he tangled heavily with a fence pole at the back of the court. He hit his leg with a loud wallop, heard a crack and slid to the ground, saying "I've broken my leg!" Everyone laughed and thought he was kidding until he yelled again "I've broken my bloody leg!" Then his mates moved!

Luckily, some had just recently finished their ambulance training so were able to apply a splint before radio-calling the ambulance and trying to contact the local doctor – who was out fishing. A friend came to the house to tell me what had happened.

We were taken by ambulance to the airport where the Flying Doctor aircraft had arrived. The pilot and paramedic made us comfortable for the trip, which was smooth. Arriving over Melbourne, the pilot descended over the wharf area so we could see the 'Spirit', which was a lovely view of the whole port. Arriving at Essendon, poor Wilf could feel every bump on the tarmac but it wasn't long before we came to a full stop.

Those fabulous flying gents transferred us to a waiting ambulance for transfer to the Royal Melbourne Hospital.

The Sister in admissions said this was the first compound fracture from playing tennis that she had dealt with, whilst other summer sports injuries were quite common.

2005 was our next experience with this fabulous service, when I had a heart attack. The Service had been changed so that King Islanders go to Tasmania rather than Melbourne. However, hours ticked by with update times and cases prioritized until at 11pm the Flying Doctor contacted King Island to say I would be going directly to Melbourne.

The next paragraph would only happen in an isolated community. The ambulance driver told my husband to 'Go home and have some sleep and we'll come and get you when we are ready to go.' We flew out to Melbourne at 12.30am and the pilot and flight nurse were great with their care.

My third experience with the Flying Doctor was in 2010. My husband was in a Melbourne respite hospital for cancer, for which there was no cure. He decided to return to the comfort of home on King Island for his last days. Within 24 hours all travel arrangements had been made with the RFDS.

The road ambulance collected us at 6.45am and delivered us to Essendon and into the care of the great Service. We were greeted and made comfortable by the team, who cared for us on our flight back to King Island. We were home by 9am, in time for breakfast!

I support the Royal Flying Doctor Service for all the wonderful work they do, right throughout Australia — especially in our corner of the nation.

A Glint of Silver in the Sky

It was December 2013. We were mustering feral goats and the day had started quite smoothly. They had mustered and yarded quite a few but my husband Paul, and son-in-law Allan, knew there must have been a 'decent' mob in the top N-E paddock because of the amount of water being consumed.

The previous evening's discussion centered on how beneficial it would be if there were three of them mustering in this particular paddock, instead of two. So, my daughter Bridie was going to join them. This meant her expressing milk for 4 month old Indiana so Grandma could care for her.

They left early in the morning with the plan to be back by lunch. I went about my business looking after little Indie. I remember her being quite disgruntled at having to take milk from a bottle and not settling very well at all. I was walking around, singing to her and patting her back when I heard Allan call me up on the UHF radio.

I acknowledged that I could hear him and then I heard the words that everyone living in the bush dreads, "Paul's had a bad accident. You need to call the Flying Doctor."

I remember asking what had happened and Allan replied with, "he's carved his face up real bad. Just call the Flying Doctor. I'm going to try and get him home."

I rang the base and relayed the message.

The base put me through to the on-call Doctor. Alistair Miller's calm and reassuring voice came on the phone and he asked a few more pertinent questions. Did I know where they were? How far from the homestead? Could I take them to Paul when they landed? Was Paul conscious?

I realized at that point that I knew what paddock they were in but had no idea of exactly where, in the 50 square kilometre paddock, they were situated. I told Dr Miller that Allan had his UHF and that I would try and raise him. Dr Miller said he would stay on the phone and listen. UHF's are great but sometimes you just cannot make contact, it all depends on whether they are in high country or not.

But, miracles happen sometimes. I called Allan up and he answered. I asked all the questions. Allan told me he was 'dinking' Paul, who was still conscious. They were trying to get to the main road in the Six Mile Paddock and that he would meet me at the Salt Creek.

He finished with the chilling words, "Just tell Dr Miller, to please hurry and get here. He's pretty bad."

When I picked up the phone all Dr Miller said was "We are on our way, Colleen."

Then I heard "Are you on channel Mum" over the UHF. It was Bridie.

I had completely forgotten about Bridie! I thought she must have been with them. Bridie was in a different corner of the paddock with her own mob of goats and had been calling and calling trying to raise her dad and husband, wondering what the hell they were doing! She had not heard anything and had no idea what had happened. Bridie asked me if I had heard from Dad or Allan at all. I didn't say too much. All I replied with was yes and just leave your goats and come home as Dad had come off his bike and they were heading back home too.

Then I thought I had better get the car ready to go and pick Paul up. I was thinking of putting a foam mattress in the back and grabbing an extra medical kit when I realized I was still walking around with dear baby Indiana asleep on my shoulder!

I continued to get the car ready still carrying Indie. Not sure why, comfort I think. Bridie arrived home and we took off to the Salt creek. We saw Allan first, shirtless and covered in Paul's blood. He had propped Paul up by the bank of the creek. Paul had Allan's shirt wrapped around his face. It was totally soaked with blood. Paul was still conscious, moaning and not able to talk very well.

We got him in the ute and headed back to the homestead. Paul seemed to be agitated and wanting the shirt removed from his face. He was indicating that it was hurting. I thought one of Indie's very soft cotton blankets might feel better, so I helped Paul to remove the shirt. I can remember looking at his injuries and thinking "Oh my God, what on Earth are they going to be able to do for you!" It was only minutes later that I heard the plane, so we headed straight to the airstrip.

The plane landed and Dr Alistair Miller, Senior Flight Nurse Barb White, Flight Nurse Angelique Galea and Pilot Neil Tucker climbed out.

It is extremely difficult to explain to someone how I felt when I first heard the drone of the plane's engine and then saw a glint of silver in the sky. That feeling of absolute relief and enormous gratitude is indescribable.

They assessed Paul and Dr Miller told us that he was taking him straight to the Royal Adelaide. Dr Miller did a lot of work for Paul on the Mahanewo airstrip. Basically trying to piece his face back, covering it, administering whatever he needed and making him comfortable. He couldn't believe that he was still conscious and remarked that adrenalin was an amazing thing.

Paul had been riding through rocky country when the accident occurred. He hit a large rock in the grass. It speared him off his bike and he then careered head-first into another rock, with the impact causing massive injuries to his face. He didn't know at the time, but he had also caused some pancreas damage and fractured two vertebrae in his spine.

Paul says he knew he had done a 'fair bit of damage' because he could actually 'hear his face breaking up as he hit the rock.'

Allan witnessed everything and did such a great job. He removed his

> *"He couldn't believe that he was still conscious and remarked that adrenalin was an amazing thing."*

shirt to try and stop the bleeding and protect the open flesh. He then got his heavily bleeding and pain-wracked father-in-law onto the back of his motorbike and set off on the long and uncomfortable ride to rendezvous with Bridie and me.

It was not an easy ride. Much of that journey was along slow and rocky terrain cutting through scrub and negotiating dry salt lakes. It was 15-20 kilometres of hell for both of them.

The RFDS plane landed in Adelaide just three hours after his crash. Paul underwent extensive tests before eventually undergoing lengthy painstaking surgery for his facial wounds. Paul's rehab was quite lengthy but he made a full recovery. The Royal Adelaide Hospital surgeons were nothing short of brilliant and everyone commented on the quality of the first response care and treatment that Paul had received from the RFDS team, on that little dirt airstrip in SA's outback.

The orthopedic person who fitted Paul for his back brace was amazed at the story and the difficult motor bike journey that followed the accident. He told Paul not to waste his money buying X Lotto tickets because he had received all his luck!

A few months later we saw Dr Miller at Port Augusta and he commented that one of the things Flying Doctors often have to confront is patients presenting with a limb or a head wrapped in towels or torn sheets. He said you quickly learn to brace yourself because usually what's underneath is pretty damn awful!

– **Colleen Manning of Mahanewo Station, SA**

> *"The orthopedic person who fitted Paul for his back brace told him not to waste his money buying X Lotto tickets because he had received all his luck!"*

They are the most amazing men and women.

My family has lived on Mahanewo Station for over 80 years and raising funds for the RFDS has always been a large focus of our lives. We have had five emergency evacuations during this period and each one makes you appreciate the dedication and wonderful support the service provides. We are not all that remote, however, two and half hours from any medical service is very daunting when you have an emergency situation.

The day my husband Paul had his accident was pretty harrowing for us all. However, the support we got from those operating the phone at the Port Augusta base and the calm and reassuring voice of the absolutely wonderful, brilliant and so sadly missed, Dr Alistair Miller, was outstanding. The follow-up care was just as exceptional. Dr Miller kept in touch throughout Paul's hospital stay but he also continually checked that Bridie and especially Allan were coping OK.

The last sentence on the RFDS logo is so very true. It absolutely provides "The finest care".

Rosella Jam

Rosella (Hibiscus Sabdariffa) is a small shrub of the hibiscus family that has a pale lemon flower followed by a succulent red calyx, which is excellent for making jams and jellies. They grow wild in the north but can also be propagated from seed.

Rosellas
Water
Sugar

Wash rosellas in a dish of water. Remove the red fleshy calyx, and the pods and save each separately. Place the pods in a saucepan, just cover with water and boil until soft. Remove from heat, strain and save the liquid.

Place the calyx in a saucepan and, using the liquid from the pods, just cover them. Simmer over heat until soft, remove and measure the volume and add an equal amount of sugar. Return to the heat and simmer, stirring occasionally, for 15 to 20 minutes. Remove and cool slightly, then bottle in sterilised jars.

If jam doesn't set, reheat and add jam setter. The pods have to be green as this indicates pectin is present. You can also make rosella cordial the same way, just add more water.

— Irene Gracie, Darwin CWA

Butterscotch Pie

Preheat oven to 180°C.

For the pastry, combine the flour, bicarb soda, cream of tartar and a large pinch of salt in a bowl. Using your fingertips, rub in the butter until mixture resembles breadcrumbs. Stir in the milk until a coarse dough forms, adding extra if required.

Turn the dough out onto a lightly floured surface and knead briefly – take care not to overwork or pastry will be tough. Form into a disc, wrap in plastic wrap and refrigerate for 30 minutes.

Roll dough out to line the base and side of a 24 cm tart tin, trimming the overhang. Line the tart shell with baking paper and fill with baking beads or dried beans. Bake for 20 minutes.

For the filling, place 2 tablespoons of the caster sugar in a small saucepan with 1 tablespoon water. Cook over medium heat for 6–7 minutes, or until a dark caramel forms. Remove from the heat and quickly add the boiling water and brown sugar, taking care as mixture will bubble and spit. Return to the heat and cook, stirring, for 5 minutes.

Combine the cornflour with 1 tablespoon water in a bowl to make a smooth paste. Add to the mixture in the pan and cook until it boils and thickens. Remove from the heat, then stir in the butter. Allow mixture to cool slightly, then stir in the egg yolks, coconut and vanilla. Pour filling into the tart shell and bake for 20–30 minutes.

Using an electric beater, whisk the egg whites in a bowl until firm peaks form. Gradually add remaining caster sugar and whisk until it is dissolved and mixture is thick and glossy. Spoon mixture over the baked tart. Bake for a further 10–15 minutes, or until meringue is light golden.

Pastry

- 1 cup plain flour
- 1¼ tsp bicarbonate of soda
- ½ tsp cream of tartar
- 75g chilled unsalted butter, chopped
- 2 Tbsp chilled milk, as required

Filling

- ⅔ cup caster sugar
- 1½ cup boiling water
- 1 cup brown sugar, lightly packed
- 1 Tbsp cornflour
- ¼ cup butter
- 2 eggs, separated
- 1 cup desiccated coconut
- 1 tsp vanilla essence

Power House Manager

Fifty years ago I took up the post of Power House Manager in the small outback town of Boulia in far western Queensland.

Included in the package were other duties like fireman, airport official, town water officer, local electrician and aircraft refueler.

It was an exciting part of my life as coming from the Gold Coast as a 22 year old with a new wife and young child I soon became familiar with many things in life I had not experienced before.

My memory of the sound of the great King Air aircraft circling Boulia before landing still echoes in my mind today.

It was one of my proudest times to first chase the kangaroos off the runway before it landed and then refuel the aircraft while the Flying Doctor held his clinic at the hospital.

The night landings were always nerve-wracking as I and some of the town people would have to light up the kerosene flares along the runway to help the pilot guide his plane for a safe landing.

I remember many times, over the next few years, how the Beechcraft King Air would circle, land and deliver the Doctor to treat and help many people in this outback country.

God bless you Flying Doctor, pilot and nurse.

– *Allan Renner*

I have written a poem that aims to convey the importance of community bonds and support. It also displays the importance of happiness and laughter as a key to tying a community together.

Magda and Keith

Escaping from the city,
I see the country red.
A landscape of fury,
Of fires not yet dead.

And yet the town is bustling,
Jovial faces all around.
Even old Magda
Is still knitting by the bound.

Old Keith still yells with merry,
Tales old, maybe true.
He tells of fishing memories,
Of crocodiles he once drew.

'Struth!' a child now exclaims,
Wonder on his face.
He not yet knows
Of Keith's embellishment
of case.

On top the child's bruised knee
Sits a plastered stripe.
A band aid placed by Keith
As he rambles through the night.

Magda knits beside
As Keith carries on.
She threads memory together,
A happy liaison.

The community is there,
To watch their special yarn.
Support that transcends darkness
And other issues born.
In the end Old Magda and Keith will look out,
With a smile not yet torn.

— Lucy Nelson-Spitzer

Biscuit Tin

As a 5 year old, the RFDS helped me but not with a medical problem!

A neighbour's station hand had been badly injured in a crash involving a motorbike versus car on a dirt road. He needed urgent medical care and transport to hospital.

This was 1980, so before the advent of satellite phones.

My mum (ex-nurse) and dad were busy getting the guy ready to move, so two other station hands were sent back to the homestead to get a hold of the RFDS on the radio.

Problem was neither knew how to work the radio and, as a year 1 School Of The Air student I was an old hand on the radio, so I was sent with them.

The boys got the biscuit tin out.

"How do we turn it on?" I turned it on – **and received a biscuit...**

"What channel for the Flying Doctor?" **Another biscuit...**

As you can imagine, I got a lot of biscuits by the time the afternoon was out.

The patient was duly collected by the RFDS and made a full recovery.

– Emma Reynolds

— **Tamara Abbott**

Here are song lyrics written by my brother Ricky Proelss. They have since been recorded by his friend Katie Crombie. Ricky lives and works as a Ringer on Stardowns Station for Appleton Pastoral Company, 75 km past Alpha, Queensland. He loves this way of life and works hard every day.

On the 1st of July last year, Ricky was in an accident where he was burned to 50% of his body. He is only here with us today because of the actions of the friends that he was camping with, the nurses from Alpha Hospital that were first on the scene and the Royal Flying Doctor Service for stabilizing him and getting him to the amazing ICU and burns team at the Royal Brisbane and Women's Hospital as quick as they could.

These words were put together by Ricky as he recovered and attended intense physiotherapy in Brisbane. We are so proud of how far he has come and he is now back working on the land, doing what he does best. I have included some photos of him back at work this year. Thanks.

Like He Can

He was just a boy, only nineteen.
Never known what places he had been.
Packed up everything he owned,
headed off on down the road,
he ain't comin' back for a while.

Four long years working on the land
with a pair of faded jeans and his
weathered hands.
Wasn't a thing he couldn't do this boy
was now a man, worth his weight
in gold.

[Chorus]
He was born to work, he was born to
try with nothing to hold him back.
He will never stop, till the day he dies,
riding down that red dirt track.
You will never meet another man who
can keep on pushing on like he can.

Got a night off to hang up his boots,
Grabbed his friends and his worn out ute.
Headed on out to the yards singin' a
song or two, all was fine, for a while.

Late that night when the stars where
out, the fire burned bright, the crickets
singing loud.
Fell into the burning flames, heard his
friends were screamin' out his name…
he was almost gone.

[Chorus]
He was born to work, he was born to
try with nothing to hold him back.
He will never stop, till the day he dies,
riding down that red dirt track.
You will never meet another man who
can keep on pushing on like he can,
like he can.

Against all odds he pulled through,
with his family there, and his friends too.
Maybe he looks different now,
he's got the scars to show just
how strong, he can be.
Pretty soon he'll be back out on the land,
with his faded blue jeans and his
weathered hands.
He's goin' down a long hard road but his
got so many places left to go and he
will with his heart on fire.

[Chorus]
He was born to work, he was born
to try with nothing to hold him back.
He will never stop, till the day he dies,
riding down that red dirt track.
You will never meet another man who
can keep on pushing on like he can,
like he can.

– Ricky Proeless

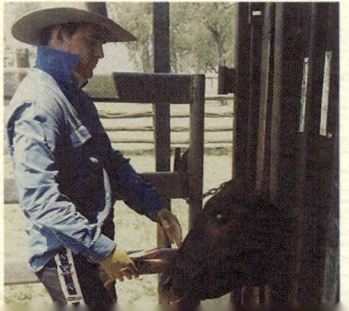

Mother-Daughter Get-Away

A mother/daughter get-away came to a complete stop at 5am on a Sunday morning.

Brooke had woken up in a panic saying she needed to vomit so I grabbed her and ran to the toilet, I put her down to stand and she collapsed. As I grabbed her she began to have convulsions. Her skin was like fire!

> "As I grabbed her she began to have convulsions. Her skin was like fire!"

I grabbed all 3 girls and rushed Brooke to the hospital. She was taken straight in with a temperature of 39.8 and heartrate of 220. She required 10 litres of humidified oxygen to bring her oxygen levels up as she was sitting at only 60%.

The doctors immediately got the cardiac team in Perth on the phone and were being guided on what to do. They gave her six doses of a medication that is supposed to slow the heart down, to reset it – but that wasn't working at all. So there was a last option to give her an electric shock to reset its rhythm, but being in a regional hospital it was not the best decision, so they advised us that they needed to get her out of there ASAP.

Brooke was flown to Perth by the Royal Flying Doctor Service and was admitted to Perth Children's Hospital. Blood test results showed she was running on very low magnesium levels so she was given magnesium which kept her heart rate at 177, which is still high but extremely better than what she was.

The next morning her heartrate was down and she was looking alert and much more responsive. The cardiac doctor on call mentioned she was having supra cardiac tachycardia and her heart was in a completely different rhythm. They were unsure how this happened but did much more over the next few days to find an answer.

> *"Every little or big part people play in this crazy, emotional rollercoaster we call our lives you make it that little bit easier for us to keep going."*

The whole ordeal was a complete nightmare, especially being in a town 8 hours away from home and on my own with the twins and a newborn – but the people involved made it so much less stressful.

Thank you to the Esperance Hospital nurses for helping keep everyone settled especially nurse Debra!

Thank you to my beautiful cousin Tammy for coming in to be with me, help, feed, hug and get Piper out to the airstrip.

Thanks to Brodie for coming in to give her some love – and my amazing best friend Kate – I would be absolutely stuck if it wasn't for you! The plane was full so we were unable to take Ash so you drove with my little girl plus your little girl 8 hours that day to get her and my car home.

Thanks Mum for meeting me at the airport with a car-seat for Piper so Brooke could be transferred to hospital and thanks to Deb for having Ashley so David could come be by his daughter's bedside.

Every little or big part people play in this crazy, emotional rollercoaster we call our lives you make it that little bit easier for us to keep going.

And if it wasn't for RFDS getting our little girl back to where she needed to be, we may not be sitting here together today as a family. Thank you.

> *"If it wasn't for RFDS getting our little girl back to where she needed to be, we may not be sitting here together today as a family. Thank you."*

– Rachael Thompson

GRASSHOPPER FEAST

– Alison Fox

In addition to the little office lizard, Trevor, a metre-long bungarra (Sand Goanna) lived under the RFDS building in Meekatharra. He was a fine specimen; handsome and proud. Most of the time, he would laze in the shade beneath our floorboards but occasionally he would saunter out into the light to sun himself or dine on insects. He did occasionally frighten unsuspecting passers-by but the staff were used to him and most visitors to the base would not have known he was there.

I was working quietly at my desk on the base one morning when Bruce phoned me to say, "Quick, come and see Trevor. He's outside here feasting on grasshoppers and there are hundreds of them."

Bruce was an RFDS pilot and he'd just returned from an overnight retrieval flight. He was preparing to put the aircraft away in the hangar when he noticed Trevor and he called me from his mobile. I took the office camera out and was delighted to snap a shot of Trevor as he passed the aircraft hangar doors. We had been inundated with grasshoppers overnight – they were drawn to the bright airport lights – and Trevor was enjoying the smorgasbord.

When the Sun Went Down

– David Thompson

I caught a Greyhound to where
the cotton grows
And lived in a shed with men
bigger than me
And drove a tractor
for a man that beat his wife
When the sun went down.

Early up with a sandwich and cooler.
Check the oil, and start it twice,
Before the dogs come running,
I jumped up into the torn seat
Just in time.

I saw the snake go under the porch
but did not say a word.
I just wondered when the
mulberries would be ripe.
And watched the orange
sun rays yawn.

Behind my tractors blue smoke
the cotton fell,
The rabbits sprung fast like they
were guilty.
My rows wandered, but I could
see that the crows were on
the corn.
So send me back home.

Time stands quiet but never silent.
And when I was far enough away
so that I could not be seen,
I turned the key to off.
And listened to the air and ate my
cheese and tomato sandwich.

I wondered on those nervous chickens
That were always walking
on eggshells.
I imagined the women in the house.
That could never leave.
Small conversations in short hand,
Of the men that came, and went,
In small circles.

I counted the rows,
I counted the crows
I counted the hours
Then the days, then the weeks
And counted my pay.

I drove the slasher over some rocks,
on the way back from the paddock
near the dam.
I packed my bag, and like a rabbit,
Sprung and waited for a Greyhound.

When the sun went down.

I am submitting a poem on behalf of my husband Michael Dickson, formerly of Hobartville Station outside of Alpha Central Western Qld. He was raised there until he left at age 28, but he misses the bush very much and this is his story in a poem.

– *Helen Dickson*

The Stockman's Life

– *Michael Dickson*

My thoughts go back to the past today,
And I find myself dreaming of my younger days.
Raised as a boy by a surrogate mum
In the outback scrub under the Queensland sun.

A little white boy with an ole black soul the only mother I knew,
So with love in her eyes she'd tell me stories of old,
She'd show me bush tucker, taught me animal tracks
And talked of a time when this country belonged to the blacks.

So in my dreams now and then when I walk that land,
I'm never alone, she's holding my hand,
Still telling me stories of long ago,
Of rituals and hunting here where the black man roamed.

So my memories today are rich
And many of my ole bush past and my old black nanny.
I still smell the gidgee and the brigalow scrub,
Hear the ole YB and the crowbar thud.

I hear the sound of a big buck roo, a dingo howl
And remember the aroma and taste of ole Tom's stew.
I remember well no man's land,
Where the brumbies dug for a drink in the sand.

Feel the warm summer breeze, see the box leaves stir,
Hear an old windmill heave with a groan and a whir,
Fresh water on tap for a thirsty stockman to drink,
After a long weary walk from an old truck on the blink.

No storm clouds that day, carting water for drought stricken stock,
Just an ole whirly whirly and the remains of an old lick block.
Hobble chains, dinner hobbles, cow bells, horse bell and
raw hide ropes, memories of my bush past.
I hear the distant voice of an old stockman wisely advising,
Save ya money son, this way of life it just won't last.

Yes it's all over now the mining booms here,
The buffles all gone, the lagoons disappeared,
No more bullocks will graze that land, it's coal country now
That's the future for man.

The ghosts of the past still haunt me today,
Sacred memories I hope never will fade,
Like thoughts of ole dogs will be with me to stay,
And my love for good horses I had on the way.

Yes they're all over now my stockman days,
My old kelly saddle weathered and frayed,
But to me that land will always be mine,
Forever in my heart, a sacred place captured in my soul and in time.

Wedding Bells

My wife and I got married on the 13th of October 2007. It's a pretty standard time of the year to get married but what made it different was that we had the ceremony in the Royal Flying Doctor Service hangar at Dubbo.

We chose the RFDS hangar at Dubbo as we wanted to get married in a place that was a little different. When the idea came up we thought it would be a great venue and not a place many people would think of!

Just to set the scene, we had a long 30m red carpet from the back of the hangar in front of the roller door, all the way to airside. There were 70 white folding chairs that were spread either side of the carpet and we had borrowed Airlinks Beech 1900 to use as the backdrop which was nosed up to the end of the red carpet. We did consider using the Kingair but at that time we only had one at the base and were not guaranteed of it being there.

My wife walked down the aisle with her dad to the theme song of the first movie they ever went to see together. A little corny but it was quite appropriate too, being the Instrumental version of the Top gun Theme song.

The whole wedding was filmed by friends of ours, Brad and Bel Cone who also did a lot of the filming for the last RFDS series that was filmed in Dubbo and Broken Hill. The video was amazingly done!!

All the wedding photos were taken around the RFDS buildings.

Our Reception was held at the Milestone Hotel in Dubbo. Again, it was another first as they had never had a wedding there. It was a great venue, and everyone had a great night!

Cheers

– **Ash Myles, RFDS pilot**

Donation

— *Vick Kandiah*

I used to work in Wirrimanu community or Balgo Hills and the RFDS used to fly on a Thursday to do its medical run.

I always remember when a member of the community gave his son $5 to buy food from the store whilst we had the local footy gathering.

The son put the $5 into the RFDS collection tin in the store instead of buying food.

SOUTHERN CROSS

— *Michael David Smart*

You meet some wonderful patients working for the RFDS.

We picked an elderly lady up from Albany a few years ago and had to wait for another patient, so we had a bit of time to chat and give the required safety briefing.

I asked if she had been flying before and she told me of her first flight when she was around 7 years old in 1932 she went for a joyflight in a big blue plane called the Southern Cross.

I was amazed and asked if Sir Charles Kingsford Smith was the pilot and she confirmed he was.

I used to work at Parafield so had seen and been in the replica of the Southern Cross aircraft so was very interested in her story. I love taking photos so I asked her if her parents took a photo of her joy flight and she replied because she was the oldest she got to go on the flight and her dad had to look after all of her brothers and sisters and were too poor to own a camera.

So I was amazed by her story.

She remembered that first flight clearly, and gave an amazing account of it. I was very grateful to have heard her story.

The Relief Is Palpable

– Leigh Cleghorn

It's 9pm, dark and cold out in the Gibson Desert, about half way between Alice Springs, Northern Territory and Kalgoorlie Western Australia.

The nurse in this remote Indigenous Community of about 200 people has asked me to help evacuate a very ill old lady.

The nurse has arranged for the RFDS to fly her patient to Kalgoorlie, the closest place she can get the treatment that may save her life. That is about 1000km or 2 days drive away, through some of the most desolate country in Australia, or anywhere pretty much.

With a dozen or so family members we drive the short distance out to the dirt airstrip, unlock the gates (the strip is fenced to keep the feral camels out) and quickly check the solar powered landing lights are on and the strip is clear of any debris.

Right on schedule the plane is heard, then its lights spotted as it banks to land and taxis to the pick-up area. The nurse and RFDS doctor quickly exchange clinical information and the old lady is transferred on a stretcher to the plane. The pilot and family members help with this. After what seems only minutes, the plane taxis to the end of the runway, turns, and kicking up dust behind, takes off and is heading Southwest to Kalgoorlie and the care the old lady desperately needs. She will be there in a couple of hours or so.

Those of us left on the ground take a deep breath as the adrenalin build up of the last hours is suddenly released. We can all relax for a bit. The old lady who is a wife, sister, mother, grandma and great friend, is in good hands, the best, and the relief is palpable.

In 30 odd years working in remote Indigenous Communities I have experienced these RFDS evacuations many times. Throughout Central Australia, (SA, WA and the NT) and the Kimberley. The location is variable but not the care, professionalism, dependability and dedication of the Service. And I include the remote area nurses in this.

So impressive it is hard to put into words without going completely over the top. I think, for me, it is best realised in that moment after the plane takes off and the patient is headed to safety. The group relief.

The understanding that when things are really hard, when life is suddenly, unexpectedly, at risk, someone is there. Then it is back to the isolation, that has its own advantages, but with the reinforced knowledge that the outside world is not so far away after all.

The Flying Doctor will always come.

P.S. As it happens, in 2014, after 25 years of these remote experiences with the RFDS, I was personally the one on the stretcher and finished up in Broome Hospital. Being the patient was an even more impressive experience. The little red RFDS clothes carry bag I was given is now one of my proudest possessions.

My Husband's Double Injury

— Claire Bousfield

In the early 1980s my husband and I were living and working in the ex-railway township of Finke, Northern Territory, which became the Aboriginal Community of Aputula when The Ghan was moved to Kulgera.

My husband was the Essential Services Supervisor and also the Garage Mechanic and Trade Trainer.

One day he was welding in the garage workshop when a drop of molten solder dropped down between his boot and his overalls, burning into his foot. That seemed to heal up but a few weeks later he accidentally cut the same foot in the place where the solder had burnt it, and unfortunately the foot got infected.

The next day he drove the community store truck to Alice Springs and became ill there and ended up in the Alice Springs hospital on antibiotics and crutches. The infection had spread systemically.

When he eventually arrived home he was still quite ill and became slightly disoriented. The Royal Flying Doctor Service was called.

The plane landed shortly after on the town airstrip and the medical team arrived at the town's medical clinic.

My husband was treated with antibiotics intravenously but the antibiotics had an adverse affect and he began hallucinating.

Fortunately the team was able to stabilize him and correct this and he was put on other medication and didn't need to be evacuated.

For the next two weeks the community's nurse trekked over to our house and gave my husband a jab in the backside. I always felt sorry for him because his birthday was spent sitting miserably on a beanbag in our living room while everyone else ate my chocolate birthday cake except him!

We are forever grateful for the quick, efficient and friendly action of RFDS – the angels of the skies.

That Feeling

After 20 years of bashing around Western Australia for the RFDS, I find it hard to remember all the different things that have happened. I have met some weird and wonderful characters along the way though.

It is a strange feeling to turn up at a primary retrieval site, being the first medical people to arrive and see the looks of relief on people's faces.

That feeling never gets old.

— Greg Phillips,
RFDS pilot Western Australia

Run-Way on Fire

I was a flight nurse with the
RFDS Mount Isa in the seventies.

We had an emergency call to an
outback station in the middle of
the night, requiring kerosene
flares to be lit so we could land.

We were operating on a small
child on the back of a ute and
one of the flares tipped over.
I remember looking up and seeing
the runway was on fire.

We quickly took the patient
on board and started take-off
procedure to get everyone
to safety.

It just so happened that we had
a visitor on board — a reporter
from a local newspaper — and as
we were taxiing on the burning
runway for take-off he turned
to me and asked if all our
emergencies were this exciting.

— *Adele Lingard*

A Different Side to Australia

I am 17 years old and I've always lived in the outer suburbs of Adelaide, South Australia, surrounded by people, buildings and noise. However, something unique and individual about myself is that I'm incredibly drawn and connected to rural Australia, as my family are fortunate enough to own a property up near the Murray River.

This is definitely one of the most influential aspects of my life, and having the opportunity to completely escape from civilisation is something I'm so grateful for.

Because of this also I have so much admiration for the small rural farming communities, plotted all around Australia and feel incredibly inspired and connected to them all.

— Felicity Lush

The work I've submitted entitled 'A Different Side to Australia' is a compilation of a variety of iconic Australian plants and flowers, representing how unique and diverse the nature and environmental side of Australia is to the rest of the world.

For this work I combined my favourite art forms together (watercolour and drawing), with my love for the Australian environment, to draw an original Australian specific plant and flower combination. As well as the illustration and watercolour painting I also included a section of hessian material to incorporate texture and an elevated element to the final piece.

The Call of the Bush

The love of the land.
Safety in the outback,
Can require a helping hand.

The Flying Doctor's been there,
For nine decades long.
Providing advice, support, assistance,
When anything goes wrong.

The Flying Doctor
might be myth and legend,
To our mates in the big smoke.
But it is a basic lifeline
For Australian country folk.

— *Kate*

Another Day at the Office...

— Kirsty Pollitt

Kirsty Pollitt, an RFDS Flight Nurse based in Alice Springs and current fixed wing Student Pilot with the Alice Springs Aero Club, recounts her experiences from a recent day out in Central Australia.

I was first on call at 0600 this particular morning and was orienting a new nurse, Nola. It was her first flying day after a week's orientation with the organisation. We were called at 0710 for a Code 2 to Pipilyatjarra (Mt.Davies) for a sick lady. It's right on Surveyor General's Corner, where Western Australia, South Australia and the Northern Territory meet. After a one hour and 50 minute flight in the magnificent Pilatus PCXII we were unable to land due to the cloud base being so low covering the tops of the hills and despite Norm's (pilot) 20,000+ hours of experience, we headed northwest and landed at Wingellina which still made for a pretty interesting landing, perfectly executed as usual.

The diversion meant that we arrived well before our patient, which gave us the opportunity to look around the great little arts centre. I found a painting that I really liked at the special price of $4000 (which included an $800 discount). Funnily enough, I left without that painting but with a much smaller one and friendlier pricing for my wallet.

Our patient soon arrived by 4WD and we departed for Alice Springs. We had an uneventful flight on the way home arriving at 1250. As we opened the door our Senior Nurse, Wendy, told us there was a Code 1 at Yulara and we needed a quick turn around. The doctor who would be accompanying us was on a flight back from Tennant Creek and he would promptly change aircraft once his patient was transferred upon arrival.

We quickly cleaned and restocked the aircraft, Norm lodged the flight plan with our cabin requirements for Ground Level pressure and as soon as the doctor landed, he inhaled his lunch and we headed off again! The approach into Yulara was nothing short of spectacular – Qantas jet popping up through the clouds below us, Uluru to the front and Kata Tjuta out to the right. Not too bad at all.

We loaded our patient, incidentally from Adelaide, who had stabilised and her situation was no longer regarded as critical. However en route back to Alice Springs at 1610 hours and about 20 minutes into the flight, the RFDS Base radioed on HF and asked us to divert to Willowra, northwest of Alice Springs on the Lander River, for a lady in early labour. I phoned the doctor at Remote Health on the

> "We were still in the climb with Nola and Dale preparing for neonatal resus on an AFT seat for a mid-flight delivery!"

satellite phone and received the patient information: The lady was 35 weeks pregnant, had received no antenatal care and was experiencing pains every 3 minutes or so, cervix was 3cm dilated and there was no midwife in the community. With the other two Alice Springs RFDS aircraft already occupied, we ensured that our current patient was stable and then diverted as requested.

We told our patient already onboard that we were diverting to Willowra and she told us that her daughter lived there and asked if we could arrange for her to come and see her on the plane. We made another satellite phone call to Remote Health and arranged for her daughter to be waiting for us on the strip. Then we had our mandatory cup of tea – who says there's no in-flight service (or entertainment)?

We also asked the Base for a strip report and what the weather was like – supposedly the airstrip was dry and the weather was 'fine'. On the approach there were horrendous, typical Central Australian storms that Norm was dodging with

expertise and there had been a lot of rain dumped near Haast's Bluff, over to Derwent Station and up to Central Mount Wedge. There was a big storm to the northeast and an even bigger one about 15 miles to the northwest rolling in very fast. I was wondering if they'd looked out the window when informing us about the weather! We do enjoy our weather radar coverage and more recently, the installation of the MFD - EGPWS system.

Norm told us we had to make this a very fast load and take-off as we'd be stuck in Willowra for 3 days if the rain hit the strip. You know the drill, red dirt + water = icky sticky mess! We landed at 1720, were met on the apron by half the community and handed over the Northern Territory News (we always take a paper to the communities). Our lady in labour was having a contraction so whilst waiting for that to finish, our patient on board and her daughter had their reunion. Two minutes later after a certain look from Norm in the cockpit and a few stern words from me that we seriously had to hurry gesticulating to the storm that looked only 2 miles away, I asked our new patient if she was pushing and she just looked at me with the look that only a woman in labour can give! Up the stairs she walked, door shut, belts buckled, headset on and we were in the take-off roll.

A minute after take off, Dale the doctor asked me if I'd, "Had a look" and I said, "No not really, I don't think I need to but there's no head yet!" After getting permission from Norm to get out of my seat, whilst in the climb, to have a look, it was action station. After the second push that I witnessed, membranes were bulging and there was a lot of hard work going on by Mum!

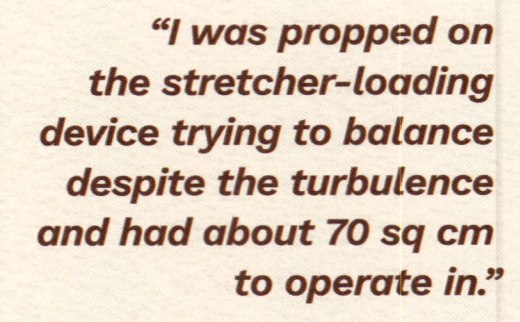

> "I was propped on the stretcher-loading device trying to balance despite the turbulence and had about 70 sq cm to operate in."

I am not quite sure how but I managed to get a delivery bundle out of the cargo net, gloved, gowned and goggled and had cord clamps and instruments ready in record time. Meanwhile at the other business end of the aircraft, Norm was dodging the "red and magenta" parts of the radar and turning up the cabin temperature until we nearly cooked (it is essential to have a warm environment for babies at birth); we were still in the climb with Nola and Dale preparing for neonatal resus on an AFT seat for a mid-flight delivery! In amongst the laboured requests for a painkiller, our first patient assured us she was fine without a hint of chest pain.

I was propped on the stretcher-loading device trying to balance despite the turbulence and had about 70 sq cm to operate in. It was going to be a golden angel baby that is born in the membrane, until I ruptured the membranes for fluid management in flight. One more grunt and out came a very hairy little head - a baby boy was born at 1734 hours at 10,500 ft. Norm radioed in to report that the number of persons on board just went from six to seven.

Congratulations were received from Melbourne Centre and aircraft on the local multicom – very exciting.

From takeoff to landing, the flight was 1hr at 17,000 ft and we even managed to clean everything up including getting everything into the correct bags, collecting some cord blood and I am proud to say that the engineers were very happy that not a single drop of blood or liquid hit the floor. As we took a minute to catch our breath, our first patient with a tear in her eye and a radiant smile told us that the new mother was her nephew's wife and that was her grandnephew just born... And they say Australia is a big country!!

After landing and handing over our patients to St John's Ambulance for the trip to Alice Springs Hospital, Nola and I had to clean up further and then go the hospital to do the Birth Certificate and write "exactly where the baby was born, if not in hospital". The registration office will get a bit of a chuckle. But working out where the baby's 'land' will be Norm's job for another day.

So, what an introduction for Nola to our working world!! Pity I hadn't told her not every day is like that day. But I was grinning like a Cheshire Cat and on a little high!! I am STILL amazed at each and every birth and the process of the miracle. WOW.

As for my own flying lessons, though the formal ones are few and far between at present, I think I have the best resource base in the world at the front of the PCXII. They really are seven of the most magnificent men in their flying machines and I am indebted to them for their patience with my never ending questioning and for them imparting little lessons every day and during those dreaded night duty flights. They too were students once and their enthusiasm with my learning is palpable. Poor Ingrid, CFI Alice Springs Aero Club, often says she tears her hair in the office watching me land a C172 like a PCXII but it's all good fun and a great way for me to learn about aviation.

Though the view from Ingrid's office might not always be as she hopes, not a single day is the same as another for me and the view from my office is pretty damn awesome!

> "A baby boy was born at 1734 hours at 10,500 ft. Norm radioed in to report that the number of persons on board just went from six to seven."

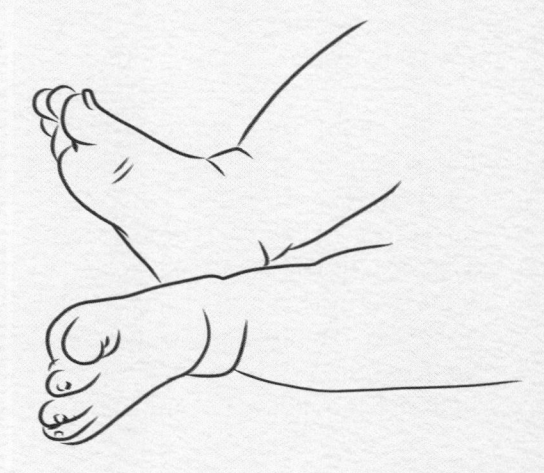

Volunteering for the RFDS

— Laura Rutherford

I volunteered with the RFDS in 2018, during my 3rd year of university.

My parents worked on stations before they had children and I'd heard all the stories about the Flying Doctor before, so when, part way through my university degree I was offered the opportunity to work with them out at a local field day, I leapt for the opportunity.

Now I'd grown up to be a little bit of a wild-child out in the sticks, where 5 o'clock Friday is non-negotiable tradition. Safety first is a thought that never enters our heads and the town consensus is we are here for a good time, not a long time.

I can count my visits to the hospital on one hand. I'm now studying in the health field, and most of what I get taught starts in the waiting room. Hardly anything is said about services to whoop-whoop where people can't, or won't, travel hours to a doctor, and certainly won't call an ambulance unless they're sure they're dying. I always wondered when we'd have a lecture about this issue.

Then along came an email titled 'Exciting Opportunity with the Royal Flying Doctor Service.' I applied immediately, despite thinking I was in with no chance as they usually send medicine, not allied health students, but lo and behold, I got in, and got on a minibus with a group of students out along the Overlander's way.

We rolled into Hughenden for the night, and here I was worrying that my jeans weren't up to the dress standard and my home-grown, down-to-earth openness wouldn't be appreciated as it's 'unprofessional'. But when the RFDS nurses turned up we all had a beer or two and my worries evaporated into a cold Northern and an even colder night sky.

We ran a 'pit stop' at the Richmond Field Day. My job was talking to the public about cancer and cancer prevention, encouraging men to check their ball bearings for lumps; and reminding women to look after their headlights.

It was staggering to see the love these people have for their aeronautically-inclined nurses. What else but love and respect could motivate them to spend time getting pricked in the finger for blood glucose instead of enjoying their hot greasy chips, watching lawnmower races and looking at the latest Kawasaki dirt bike?

Those ladies I worked with remain among the most inspirational I've met, and it almost breaks my heart to think how grateful they were that we turned up to help out. Surely these amazing men and women of the air should be receiving more assistance than they know what to do with. Their laid-back attitude and their respect for their patients made me re-evaluate everything I had been taught, because I'd finally learned exactly what healthcare should be. It isn't about the clinicians who fix injuries, it's about the smiling faces that enrich lives in some of the harshest places in Australia.

The impact of the RFDS that I experienced could be written with a lot of long words, but a more concise and probably more accurate description was an interaction with a miniscule child, only 2 or 3 years old, who came over to answer a question for a sticker with which to earn a showbag. Up he came, accompanied by an older sibling, so we asked him the all-important question — "If mummy or daddy get hurt, who do you call?" "The Flying Doctor" he said, as if stating something as obvious as the drought that has been ravaging the country.

Clearly we were all idiots, and he toddled off with his sticker, glad to be away from these city slickers who didn't know anything about how people survive in the country.

Grateful

Without the RFDS my hubby and my kids' daddy might not be here today.

For some this post might be confronting but it is my prayer that it will awaken you to the need to listen to and respond to symptoms your body shows you – as it may just save your life!

Our morning started with an abrupt wakeup call when Tim got up to go to the toilet – nothing out of the ordinary here; however, when he went to go back to sleep he was jolted awake with heart palpitations, chest and arm pain, clammy skin and cold extremities.

I immediately noticed the glazed look in his eyes and called 000.

They responded so efficiently and did a brilliant job as first responders. It was clear that with a resting heart rate of 250bpm, (which later reached an unfathomable 300bpm) that something was not right and we were told he could go into cardiac arrest. Back-up paramedics were called and Tim was whisked away to our local hospital with lights flashing.

After calling and waking up a close friend to ask her to watch the kids, I followed closely behind in a second ambulance.

> *"I never thought I would hear the words, 'Clear, Shock' in all of my days. I can still hear the thump, thump of his body being shocked, but this movie scene had become our reality."*

Photo: Facebook post May 5, 2016

Upon arrival, Tim was given some medicine to try and chemically return his heart rhythm to normal but this failed. They needed to use the defibrillator. I never thought I would hear the words, "Clear, Shock" in all of my days. I can still hear the thump, thump of his body being shocked, but this movie scene had become our reality. Thankfully, this reality meant Tim now had a normal heart rhythm.

Tim did not lose consciousness but his heart was not working properly. He was admitted to the High Dependency Unit and they suspected he had Wolff-Parkinson-White syndrome and Atrial Fibrillation on top of that. His whirlwind ride did not stop there as he was transported to Wesley Hospital in Brisbane by the unsung heroes of the Royal Flying Doctor Service.

Cardiologists had to assess him. The kids and I remained at home to sustain some normality.

We were emotional and sad because we missed Tim but we were elated that he is still with us. All because we didn't ignore the signs. All because medical professionals were able to do their job and do it well. All because the RFDS could get Tim to a metropolitan hospital with heart specialists. All because we listened to the signs.

Tonight my kids still have a daddy and I still have my soul mate!

– Shelly Kerr

TWICE LUCKY

It was rare to see any vehicles at all on that lonely road, let alone one hunkering down on two flat tyres – with two people inside.

Working for the RFDS, you know your job will entail assisting people when things go wrong. In my time as a base pilot at Meekatharra in remote Western Australia, I flew the plane as part of a team involved in all sorts of medical rescues and patient retrievals. It was very satisfying work. But my wife and I did not expect to come to the aid of people in trouble on a day off, well away from our working lives.

We have an old Land Rover Defender and we love to take it off the beaten track whenever there's a chance. One winter's weekend, we packed our swags and set off to explore ghost towns, abandoned railways and disused roads in lonely country to the east of Meekatharra. We spent a couple of nights out there, listening to dingoes howl, gazing at the stars and cooking over campfires. We didn't see another soul, nor did we expect to.

Our plan that particular weekend, with the help of an old map, was to find and hopefully follow a road that had not been used since the early 1930s and we had travelled a couple of hundred kilometres, criss-crossing back roads and station tracks, to initially locate it. We hoped we may be able to follow the old road at least part of the way back towards Meekatharra but the going was much rougher than expected, with sizeable termite mounds and trees growing between the tyre tracks. After a while, the road became impenetrable and to our disappointment, we had to abandon our mission and drive back the way we'd come – travelling more than 200 kilometres further than we'd hoped.

It was late in the day when we finally turned onto the modern dirt road that would lead us back to Meeka and we headed into the setting sun, throwing a long shadow and a huge plume of dust behind us. We were just discussing the dropping temperature and reaching for our coats when I first noticed an old vehicle off to the side of the road. Initially we drove past, thinking it was another abandoned wreck, but on reflection I realised something wasn't quite right with the way the vehicle was sitting and we decided to go back and investigate.

On approach I saw that both the rear tyres had been shredded and so had the spare – that car wasn't going anywhere – but the biggest surprise

– *Bruce Carroll*

was that two people were sitting inside, a middle-aged man and a young lad of eight or ten. They were very pleased to see us and told us they'd been there for more than seven hours. They'd given up on seeing another car that day and were preparing to weather the night out there.

It turned out that the man was taking his mate's son, Jack, from a town in the WA Goldfields to see Jack's dad, a patient at Meekatharra Hospital, but they expected the road to be sealed all the way and were caught out when they found it to be stony and heavily corrugated. Their tyres – in fact their whole vehicle – really wasn't suited to the conditions and in no time, the tyres began disintegrating. They were well beyond repair and our spares didn't fit their car.

The man was anxious because he didn't want to leave the vehicle, which he'd borrowed from a friend. He felt he should stay with it and asked us if we could send help by arranging to send spare tyres out from Meeka when businesses opened the next morning. His greatest concern, however, was Jack. The lad had no warm clothes and they had no food and little water with them. Once he learned that we worked for the RFDS, he said he felt he could trust us and asked if we'd deliver the boy to his father in town, a further 180km on, and we agreed. Leaving food and water with the man, we loaded Jack in with us and set sail towards Meeka once more.

As we were about to drive off, the man said, "You know, this is the second time the RFDS has rescued young Jack."

"What happened, Jack?" I asked.

"Well," a timid Jack replied, "I fell into a glass fish tank once and the glass broke and nearly cut me in half." He lifted his shirt to show a thin red scar running around his ribcage. "Killed the fish too, it did!"

Broke My Back

– Andy Salter

In 1992 I fell 22 feet and broke my back while working in the Cooper Basin.

We had a Royal Flying Doctor Service medical chest on site – thank goodness.

My work colleagues strapped me up and the RFDS aircraft landed. The flight nurse came running across with a needle in her hand and asked "Where do you want it?". "Anywhere!", I replied.

After that I was out of it. They flew me to Port Augusta and x-ray showed two broken vertebrae. They then flew on to Adelaide.

They saved me.
Magnificent team work.

Cheers RFDS

Under the Wing

– Helena Mead

Millicent is a small but busy country hospital, almost smack bang between Adelaide and Melbourne, each being 400 and something kilometres away. It is that sort of regional hospital where you know most, if not all the nurses and doctors by first name. If they weren't at your last BBQ, you would have almost certainly bumped into one of them at the shops.

My 80 year old mother had been admitted, yet again, however this time her condition needed the specialist equipment of a city hospital so help by way of the Flying Doctor was called upon.

The response was quick and before we knew it Mum was being strapped to a gurney in the caring hands of the retrieval team and taken by ambulance to the airstrip.

It was a dog of a night; the rain was sweeping in sideways as the small plane took off. We felt relieved that within an hour Mum would be receiving the specialist care she needed.

Unbeknown to us at the time, the Flying Doctor received a call on their way to Adelaide and took a short detour to Ceduna, to pick up another patient. As the plane landed at Ceduna, Mum found herself uncomfortably in need to relieve herself. With no toilet on board and no amenities available at that late hour, she was escorted out of the plane to the only available spot – under the wing of the plane. Was she horrified? No! She laughed along with the team as they carefully helped her aboard saying there was no need to flush as the rain would see to that. Thanks to their care and dedication, Mum received the attention she needed and laughed every time she recalled her story.

First Responder Uncle Herb

The Heroes of my story are my Uncle Herb Hemley, Tom Hunter, Cobar Ambulance and the Royal Flying Doctor Service. But l will begin at the beginning and introduce you to my wonderful Uncle Herb.

Herb Hemley at the age of 84 is the Honorary Mayor to Tilpa and has completed his Probationary Constable Training in 2014 at the age of 80.

Tilpa is in Outback NSW and is located on the Darling River which boasts a population of 9 fantastic people. Uncle Herb was recently seen playing cricket on Landline for a story on the Darling River and he is also featured in an ad for an iconic NSW outback tourist scene, with a photo that ended up being published in the Readers Digest. So, here is the story:

A couple of years ago my parents were visiting my Uncle Herb, dad's brother in Tilpa, NSW.

One night as my parents, David and Shirley where watching TV in Uncle Herb's humble adobe, Uncle Herb stumbled in after a few beers at the Tilpa Hotel calling out "Where's my medical kit – where's my medical kit?"

My parents were not sure what was happening at this time but watched on bemused as Uncle Herb was rummaging quickly though his first aid kit – bandages flying in and out of the kit of medical paraphernalia.

Uncle Herb called out "Shirl get me a towel". An old towel sat on the back of the chair where my mum sat, so she handed Uncle Herb that one to him.

Uncle Herb turned to his mate Tom who had stumbled in with him and yelled out "Tom fill the esky – it's going to be a long night!" Tom knew that fill the esky meant fill it with ice and beer.

My parents still had no idea what was happening. My father said it all happened too quick to ask questions.

Uncle Herb & Tom drove 50 kilometres out of town, down a rough dark road to a working station. The young man's mother had wrapped towels around his neck to stem the bleeding. He had ridden his bike into a barb wire fence at throat level, creating a deep cut.

A phone call was placed to the Cobar Ambulance who made the 200km drive out to the station. Carefully the ambulance staff began the process of stabilising the patient for the 50kms back into Tilpa to the airstrip.

Back in Tilpa an hour had passed and an airplane could be heard. The Royal Flying Doctor Service had arrived and was patiently waiting for the ambulance to arrive.

Those who attended this man at the station believed the young man might die from his injuries; however because of the medical attention given by the Cobar Ambulance and Royal Flying Doctor Service they were able to slow the bleeding and stabilise him. They saved his life.

He was flown to Broken Hill for full medication attention. Had it not been for the team effort of the entire assembly of helpers the outcome would have been very different. The patient has recovered and gone onto return to his working life at the station.

Sometime later my parents were visiting the Broken Hill Royal Flying Doctor Service base. My father asked if they knew Herb Hemley from Tilpa and they replied with a grin "We certainly do!"

– Lisa J Hemley

Service for Travellers

We were travelling up the Strzelecki Track in remote South Australia and had two tyre blow-outs that kept us at the Mungerannie Hotel camping area, for over a week.

The RFDS flew in a group of about nine student dental technicians and a supervisor. They were there to check teeth for anyone in nearby stations as well as travellers. We had had our teeth checked before our trip but there were at least 21 locals who came in for this service. We were mighty impressed.

Before Mungerannie we had been in Maree over Easter. We met the RFDS nurse on duty. Asked if she did flu shots as we were going to a large birthday party on our return and didn't want to risk catching bugs there. She said yes of course she could. We offered to pay for the serum but were told it was unnecessary – so we asked where the RFDS donation box was and put our money in there instead.

Bless you all.

– Marianne Boot

Saving Reverend John Flynn

I believe the following tale to be true.

I took my elderly father from Melbourne to Colac, Victoria to have lunch with his brother and they were reminiscing about their early lives in Beech Forest (my father was born in 1887).

They mentioned the name John Flynn and I jokingly said "wasn't he 'Flynn of the Inland'?"

To my astonishment they both said yes he was a minister at Beech Forrest (a fact I didn't know but later checked and confirmed was true).

So they then told me this story.

Reverend John Flynn operating a pedal radio

John Flynn was leaving Beech Forest for another posting. He was attempting to cross the flooded Aire River on horseback and got into considerable difficulties.

My grandfather, Charles Edward Hall, who was a very good horseman, went into the river and returned John Flynn safely to the river bank. He then helped him to cross the river safely.

Fascinating story. I guess one could say that if it hadn't been for my grandfather getting him safely across that flooded river, the Royal Flying Doctor Service would not have come to be on the 17th of May 1928.

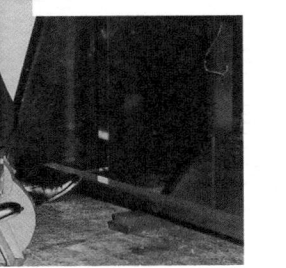

– Selwyn Hall

Help From Strangers

– Rose Slade

I was evacuated in 1992 when I went into labour at 26 weeks pregnant.

I was living in a remote community Pipalyatjarra in South Australia.

After a 3 hour journey in the back of a Toyota on dirt roads, with the local nurse trying to stabilise me, we arrived at the evacuation air strip.

The Warakurna community had turned out in force to light up the airstrip so the plane could land. It makes me cry when I think of it.

I never knew who those people were and never got to thank them for turning out at two in the morning. I had an infection but my pregnancy ended well and a beautiful healthy child was born two months later.

Thank you everyone

Esmeralda Rolls

75 g cold unsalted butter
250 g self-raising flour
1 tsp baking powder
1 heaped tsp caster sugar
125 mL milk
¾ cup golden syrup
2 Tbsp desiccated coconut
1 cup boiling water

Preheat oven to 190°C. Generously grease a 30 x 20 cm baking dish.

Sift the flour, baking powder and a large pinch of salt into a bowl. Using your fingertips, rub in the butter until the mixture resembles breadcrumbs. Add milk gradually to make a soft dough.

Turn the dough out onto a lightly floured surface and knead briefly to bring it together. Roll the dough out into a 30 x 12 cm rectangle and spread 2 Tbsp of the golden syrup over the dough. Roll up dough starting at one long side to form a log and cut it into 10 even-sized pieces. Arrange the pieces cut-side up in a single layer in the dish.

Combine the remaining golden syrup, coconut and the boiling water in a saucepan and bring to a simmer. Pour over the rolls in the dish so that the mixture reaches two-thirds of the way up the rolls (it's important that you do not completely cover the rolls).

Bake for 45 minutes to 1 hour, or until the rolls are golden and cooked through and the sauce is thick and syrupy.

First Flight as a Locum RFDS Medical Officer, 1966

– Bill Pigott

I am a retired medico living in Berry NSW, following a 21-year career with the World Health Organisation. My clinical undergraduate training was at Sydney Hospital and I worked there for 6 years following graduation in 1965. Dr Norman Rose, Superintendent of Sydney Hospital at the time, was also President of the NSW Section of the RFDS.

In 1966 Dr Rose arranged for selected Sydney Hospital Medical staff members to do locums, while the Service was without a second medical officer. I was privileged to be the first one and was fortunate to be able to do several.

The learning began on my second day in Broken Hill. We flew to Tibooburra in a small de Havilland Drover (an Australian built version of a Canadian aircraft with three engines, one on the nose and one on each wing).

Flying across what they call the 'dead heart' of Australia, there were four of us, Jack Jenkins the pilot, Graeme Ambrose the regular Flying doctor, Ted Eslake the dentist and myself. Graeme Ambrose was taking me out to a routine clinic at the Tibooburra Hospital to introduce me to the work I would be doing for the next four weeks while he was away on leave.

Seen from the air, the land below us is red. It is almost formless. There are small hills but, on the whole, it is flat and open. We fly across this for an hour and a half or more to reach the small town of Tibooburra. Working together, the clinic took about two hours. Towards the end, our pilot came several times to the door to ask "have you finished yet?" Dr Ambrose, would reply "No", and the pilot would respond "Come on, we have to get moving". He certainly seemed agitated about something.

> "He pointed out through the window, where instead of the clear blue sky of the Australian outback, all we could see was red from floor to ceiling."

These clinics always ended with a cup of tea and splendid refreshments with the nurses who staffed these tiny hospitals way out in the middle of nowhere. Such morning and afternoon teas were legendary and are stories in themselves. However, on this occasion, no sooner had we started our tea and sandwiches, Jack appeared and said "We have to go. We cannot waste any more time. No sandwiches. Drink your tea quickly. We really do have to go". He pointed out through the window, where instead of the clear blue sky of the Australian outback, all we could see was red from floor to ceiling. There was a dust-storm approaching. Jack the pilot says we have to go, so we go.

As we took off from the small dirt airstrip, I realized that this dust-storm was between us and our destination, the base at Broken Hill. We actually flew into the dust, pilot, doctor, dentist and myself the locum doctor, together in the small cabin of this valiant de Haviland Drover aircraft. Jack seemed to be a bit unsettled and soon announced he would see if we could get above the dust. He puts the aircraft into a climb, however as we reach our limit, the engines seem to falter. He announces "We cannot get above the dust, and so we will try to go below it."

By this time, it is clear to me that he has also lost radio contact with our base, and with anyone else. He could not get below the dust either. The dust-storm was down to the ground.

For an hour, or so it seemed to me, we flew around, sort of blind, sort of looking for something. Graeme Ambrose explained that Jack was looking for some recognizable landmark so that he could locate our position, but clearly was not finding it. I found myself just looking out the window, looking at all this dust and realizing we were quite close to the ground. Strange and curious. A new experience for me. I suspect I was a little bit tense by this time, however I knew this to be so when the dentist, Ted Eslake, well known for his dry sense of humour, says "Look, Jack's taken his hat off, so he must be really worried".

They explained that Jack Jenkins, a most experienced bush pilot, always wore a hat, and only ever took it off when he was really worried!

As I continued to look out the window, I found myself consciously accepting that there was nothing I could do. I said to myself that he is the pilot, he has the skill to get us out of this. I said to myself that I must let go and let him do what he has to do and get us out of here. "He has as much interest in getting out of this as I do" I told myself. So that is what I did. I remember that I actually relaxed and began to feel strangely calm. Soon Jack found a fence, which he followed and came to a road, which he announced he recognised. He was able to raise the homestead he knew to be nearby, one with an airstrip, on the radio. We turned and followed the road, found the airstrip landed safely and spent the night at the homestead.

Since that day, flying in small aircraft has not seemed to bother me, although as a child I hated flying and would get terribly airsick. Later, when working in the highlands of Papua New Guinea, and much later in Nepal, I was often in single-engined aircraft, landing and taking off on some of the most incredible airstrips, but was never worried about flying. I seemed to have a capacity to let go and let the other person, the person whose job it was, take the responsibility for their work. The dust storm had been a significant learning experience for me.

...

One morning, one of the calls was from a cattle-station some 200 miles away from the base in Broken Hill. It was the mother of a 15-year-old lad with pain in the abdomen, who was feeling very sick and had vomited a couple of times.

It sounded to me that it might be appendicitis. Normally as a doctor one would talk with the patient and do a physical examination. You would feel the abdomen to find out if the pain is localised and where it is most intense. I would have also tested for what is called 'rebound tenderness'. To do this, you press in on the abdomen and let go quickly. If the pain is more intense when you let go, this is a sign of inflammation within the abdominal cavity.

It was not possible for me to do any of this by radio, so I thought, "maybe I can get the mum to do that for me". Speaking to her on the radio, I asked her was she near the patient. "No, he's in the other room. Over". I asked her to test for tenderness with the flat of her hand. She had to leave the radio, go to the patient. She returned to say it was really tender in the lower right corner. I then asked her to press on the lower part of the abdomen and let go quickly. She came right back and said "Yes, he really cried out when I let go quickly. Over to you doctor." My suspicion is confirmed. I found myself thinking, "Isn't that interesting. Here is a mother, probably of basic-level education, who is able to elicit a key clinical sign for me".

The lad will need to come in to the hospital in Broken Hill by plane as soon as possible. I phone the pilot from the radio desk and he tells me we can get out there in an hour and half. I calculate that by the time we've got to the plane, fly out and back, and get the lad into hospital, it would be 4 hours or more. This would be long enough for the effects of any pain medication to wear off in time for his assessment by the hospital doctors, which meant he could have something immediately for the pain.

So I now did another thing that would be quite unusual in any setting. I asked the mother, by radio, to go to the medical chest (which each household has as part of the Flying Doctor Service set-up, containing a range of medications, including injections, each with its own number), to take an ampoule of a particular number, and give a particular amount as an injection into the lad's upper arm muscle. I was asking her to give her son an intramuscular injection of morphine, to deal with the pain until he got to the hospital.

What I had done here was to enable another person to take responsibility for what, in a normal hospital or clinic setting, would have been mine. I would have taken all responsibility for the diagnosis, and the initial treatment. However, under these circumstances, we had to share that responsibility. It was a real eye-opener for me to see how much you can, if you have the right setup and you have no choice, actually enable another person to take responsibility for what would otherwise be highly professional technical tasks. I was amazed by the extent to which these ordinary folk, out in the country, in these way-out areas in the Australian outback, can with the help of a doctor on a radio, take responsibility for things such as making a diagnosis and administering appropriate medication.

...

The whole four weeks of locum work with the RFDS proved to be a wonderful experience for me. The Royal Flying Doctor Service gave me, as a 24 year old back in 1966, the opportunity to learn some most valuable personal lessons about 'Responsibility', letting those who have a responsibility carry out that responsibility and when necessary enabling others to take or share responsibility. I look back and realise my life has been better for having done so. In addition, I discovered the extraordinariness of people we consider to be ordinary.

"It was a real eye-opener for me to see how much you can, if you have the right setup and you have no choice, actually enable another person to take responsibility for what would otherwise be highly professional technical tasks."

Miracles Do Happen

– *Christine Simon*

When Mum and Dad bought a 120 acre farm at Myrrhee about 30 miles south west of Wangaratta, Victoria, they brought with them their 5 young children, me being the youngest at only 3 years of age.

They moved to that farm in 1945. Life was quite a struggle, not much money and the farm a bit run down. Dad set about clearing and cutting down gum trees with cross cut saws, Dad on one side of the tree and my oldest brother the other side of the tree. They would saw and saw till the tree came crashing down. Those logs were dragged by a Clydesdale horse and put across a deep gully with a creek below to help mend a partly washed away bridge. They worked for many months to get it strong so we could get to the other side and gather walnuts in the orchard.

To move around on the farm, with no tractor, Dad would harness up the horse and hook it to a sledge. Us kids would sit on and get a ride — such fun.

On one occasion Dad had to disc plough a large plot of land to plant corn for his pigs. Dad, being poor didn't have a watch to wear, so Mum wrapped her silver watch in a white linen handkerchief and put it in a little white leather purse with a snib. She gave it to Dad to put in his pocket so he knew the time to come home for lunch.

On one day he went to take the watch out of his pocket, it wasn't there, he was in deep shock; he had lost it in the ploughing. He was so sad when he came home for lunch and had to tell Mum that he'd lost her watch. They were so upset as that was Mum's only jewellery and was given to her as a wedding present.

Life goes on, working on the farm. Dad, with the help of the two eldest boys milked 20 cows by hand night and morning. Life was hard doing the many farm chores required.

Months passed and the following autumn, that large plot of land was being ploughed again with horse and disc plough. Dad was walking home for lunch over the turned stony earth when he saw what he thought was a whitish stone. He picked it up and to his amazement it was the little leather purse.

He couldn't believe his eyes.

The stitching had all rotted away, the handkerchief had rotted at all the folds and fell in bits as he opened it up. He found the glass was still intact but the face of the watch was fairly rusty. Mum and Dad couldn't believe it could be in the ground for many months and be found the following year.

Mum soaked the watch in kerosene for quite some time, and believe me, she got the watch going and wore it for several years, until Dad bought her a gold watch for one of their big anniversaries.

Remote Northern Territory in the 60s

Here is a photo from the 60s of a plane labeled Northern Territory Medical Service which was part of the broader Royal Flying Doctor Service.

This picture was taken in January 1961 at the Areyonga Settlement – a small town in the Northern Territory located about 220 km west of Alice Springs. It has a population of about 195, most of whom are Aboriginal. The people are mostly Pitjantjatjara, with some Arrernte and Walpiri families. The town is governed by Areyonga Aboriginal Community.

My father was farm manager and my mother worked at the hospital, which in those days was generally located in the worker's kitchen.

The photo shows, the pilot (with cap) Harry Moss and a taller gentleman, Dr Emminson. In the plane doorway is myself, and the two boys are the sons of a local staff member.

– *Margaret Freeburn (Davidson)*

Nubblegum

Here is my personal short story relating to the beginning of my Leukaemia journey and subsequent bone marrow transplant.

"It's looking more likely you'll have to go to Brisbane for further testing, it could be a couple of weeks down there" reiterated yet another of the emergency department personnel.

In a bid to shine some light on the darkening whirlwind of the moment, my wife shares with me the musings of our five-year-old daughter on the way to prep this morning.

"Mum, what rhymes with bubblegum?"

"Uhh hmmmm…..not sure, darling", distractedly replied Jen, clearly not realising the potential for bubblegum related creative genius.

"Nubblegum!" states Dusty, matter of factly with a sprinkling of that childhood excitement that can't be bought.

Back in the eye of the storm, I erupt in tears of joy, laughter and the excruciating pain delivered with it, defining the moment our journey begins.

As we take to unknown skies in the Royal Flying Doctor Service, I know that everything will be ok and I'll do whatever it takes for those that await.

— Gavin Hill

STRUTH – THIS CAN'T BE REAL!

— Marg Haebich

Settled, unsettled or just resolve! It's hard to describe where we are now. That anguish was bound by a coping numbness for some months.

No one had expected such a threatening disaster in Beechmont, Queensland. The plateau of Beechmont nurtures a wonderful community of people. The world heritage listed Lamington National Park is its backdrop, along with some of the most spectacular sunrises and sunsets forming other brilliant views. Pristine air is filtered by mounded blankets of green and familiar scents of the Australian bush. Homes are placed to optimise this beauty with the never-ending hills of the Great Divide. Genuine friendships are well nurtured feeding our heart and soul, and this is ever so present when the community celebrates or is in need.

This need began with a whisper and built with relentless, self-fuelling ferocity on the morning of September 6th, 2019. This was a school day for me. My husband kept me posted with regular updates of fires in the valleys below, fires too close to my son and his family. It was the first time it felt so real.

I was not my usual self – trying hard to distract my students from the settling smoke around our school. Spot fires and controlled burns were relentlessly feeding the ever-thickening haze. School break was now indoors as both students and teachers struggled to breathe.

Fortunately, it was after school when I had word of helicopters flying over to smother an out-of-control 'controlled' burn before an impending wind change. My husband was keen for me to get home, particularly worried about our son, his beautiful wife and our precious grandchildren.

The deep gorge of Lamington National Park, across from Timbarra Drive where they lived, now had strong winds roaring through. This perfect setting for my son, his family and menagerie of animals was clearly under threat. Now home, the smell of smoke was heavy, and a feeling of relief overwhelmed when I saw my daughter-in-law's car with the grandchildren. She too had become nervous of the closeness of the fire packing the car with as many treasures as she could.

> *"Spot fires and controlled burns were relentlessly feeding the ever-thickening haze. School break was now indoors as both students and teachers struggled to breathe."*

I went into Mama mode setting up their rooms and starting dinner to normalise things. We were anxiously waiting for our son, who spent much of the day blocking and filling gutters with water, clearing rubbish and closing everything as airtight as possible. He madly packed his musical equipment, a shed full of tools and the dogs. He then let out the chooks so they could find their own protection. With adrenalised strength and a heavy heart, he joined us at what was then a safe haven from potential fire. Every form of communication was now our focus as we waited to hear updates.

Timbarra, Binna Burra and its surrounds were now evacuating fast. Our brigades were deeply concerned at how complex the fires were becoming. The 'controlled' burn at Sarabah, was now a maze of wind-changing tracks of fire, licking their way through every available source of fuel. The winds changed too quickly for our meteorologists and fire controllers, with areas too dangerous to access. Decision making was severely tested.

Rural crews were stretched trying to manage each fire that neared someone's home. For the first time, Binna Burra mountain and its historical lodge were under serious threat. Tourists and workers were evacuated. Even at this point, long-time residents still held onto local knowledge. 'Surely the surrounding rainforest would protect it?' None of us even thought to account for rising temperatures that had changed our weather conditions, flora and fauna. 'Remember when we had four relentless weeks of heavy rain and fog?' 'Remember when you'd only see black cockatoos- not noisy, largening flocks of white ones!'

'Struth... this can't be real!' News was in of the fire hitting Timbarra Drive. We were relieved the family were with us, but with white faces and nervous fidgets, growing worry had cemented.

I distracted all with food, bath-time bubbles, cuddles and calming bedtime stories with our precious grandchildren. They sensed our unease and what was at stake. The elder of the two was wide eyed and keen to share how smoky it was at his place and how busy mummy had been packing all their things in the car. I reassured him that all the fire fighters were working hard to protect their home, and even feeding their chooks! Satisfied, he and his brother eased into a restful sleep.

As evening wore on, whisperings of 'struth' fed feelings of dread. News

> *"As evening wore on, whisperings of 'struth' fed feelings of dread. Seasons worth of fuel and winds that gained momentum tore through the valley and inflamed all the beautiful bushland around and right through their street."*

was coming in fast that houses were lost on Timbarra Drive and the historical Binna Burra lodge was under fire. Seasons worth of fuel and winds that gained momentum tore through the valley and inflamed all the beautiful bushland around and right through their street.

My son and his wife were convinced their place would be damaged at the very least. They were relieved that they salvaged as many treasures as possible, but what were they about to face?

By next morning, authorities made it very clear the whole area was closed off as it continued to be unsafe. With little sleep, my son awoke with an urgency to see what remained of their home. Reports were mixed, nine homes damaged. No eleven, one of many challenges to come as our firies were still trying to assess the damage. At one point, rumours were trickling in that our son's home had perished. Another, that it was damaged.

"It was heartbreaking seeing news reports of wide-eyed residents, huddled in lines, grasping each other in the pursuit for answers and trying to put on a brave face through the sea of cameras and well-meaning support staff."

More frustration and yearning to know. Well-meaning authorities delayed informing some residents for weeks following the fire. This created a slow-building cancer of stress which prevented their minds settling into a direction of resolve to move forward.

It was heartbreaking seeing news reports of wide-eyed residents, huddled in lines, grasping each other in the pursuit for answers and trying to put on a brave face through the sea of cameras and well-meaning support staff. My son and his family soon to join this line to the unknown.

With the help of like-minded friends and a relenting police officer, my son saw his home. There was damage to the exterior, and the fire ate its way into the study where a smog of charcoaled damage and ash prevailed. Homely furnishings and years of memories became a carpet of grey ashen- snow. The smoke and water damage were relentless. My daughter-in-law's true strength shone through here. Her treasures were lost, including a cherished old sewing machine from her grandmother, now charred and melted, and her hand-crafted dream catchers an ashen mess. She had focused on everyone else, leaving these behind...heartbreaking.

As my son was escorted out of the street, the haze and heat revealed an eeriness of lifeless silence. The gorge side revealed sharp silhouettes of scorched remains, smells of molten metal and plastic and hues saturated in grey. Seeing now what others had lost, saddened him. Gratitude then overcame, as he had something left.

"As my son was escorted out of the street, the haze and heat revealed an eeriness of lifeless silence. The gorge side revealed sharp silhouettes of scorched remains, smells of molten metal and plastic and hues saturated in grey."

When my son returned home to show us the damage, his strength and humility empowered us. He carried a sense of peace, satisfied with what he was dealing with. His focus became caring for those around him and moving forward. I did the same and spent time supporting an astonishing group of women from the Beechmountain Queensland Country Women's Association, feeding our exhausted firies. Our new normal was seeing them with their tired eyes smudged in soot and uniforms dressed in flakes of ash. I arrived when food preparation and delivery was well underway. These women had worked for more than twenty-four hours without sufficient sleep yet were driven by sheer determination to support our community to enable it to survive.

It was an honour to feed and thank the very people who had saved my son and his family's home. I was able to pass on regular updates of how the children's chooks were faring. Their chooks, and many other animals, survived on bundled, leftover scraps that the Firies took with them on their patrols. Such a simple gesture resonated with our community. Other community members and government groups kicked into gear with further food preparation, passing on more direct support to families in need of shelter and services. This continued for months, well after the fires were controlled.

It was humbling to see how my family were supported by friends and the community when it came to clean up and planning the rebuild of their home. Around thirty volunteers turned up with every cleaning item imaginable and worked their way through the destruction. The clean-up was a stark reminder of the devastation but enlightened by the kindness and generosity to help them rebuild their lives. Still today, their beautiful house is nearly a home once more. Only the laundry roof and blackened trees remind us of that fateful night. Through the help of so many, that eventful moment in time drew strength, resilience and resolve.

Struth! You can't ask for more than that!

"The clean-up was a stark reminder of the devastation but enlightened by the kindness and generosity to help them rebuild their lives."

DROP IN POSSUMS

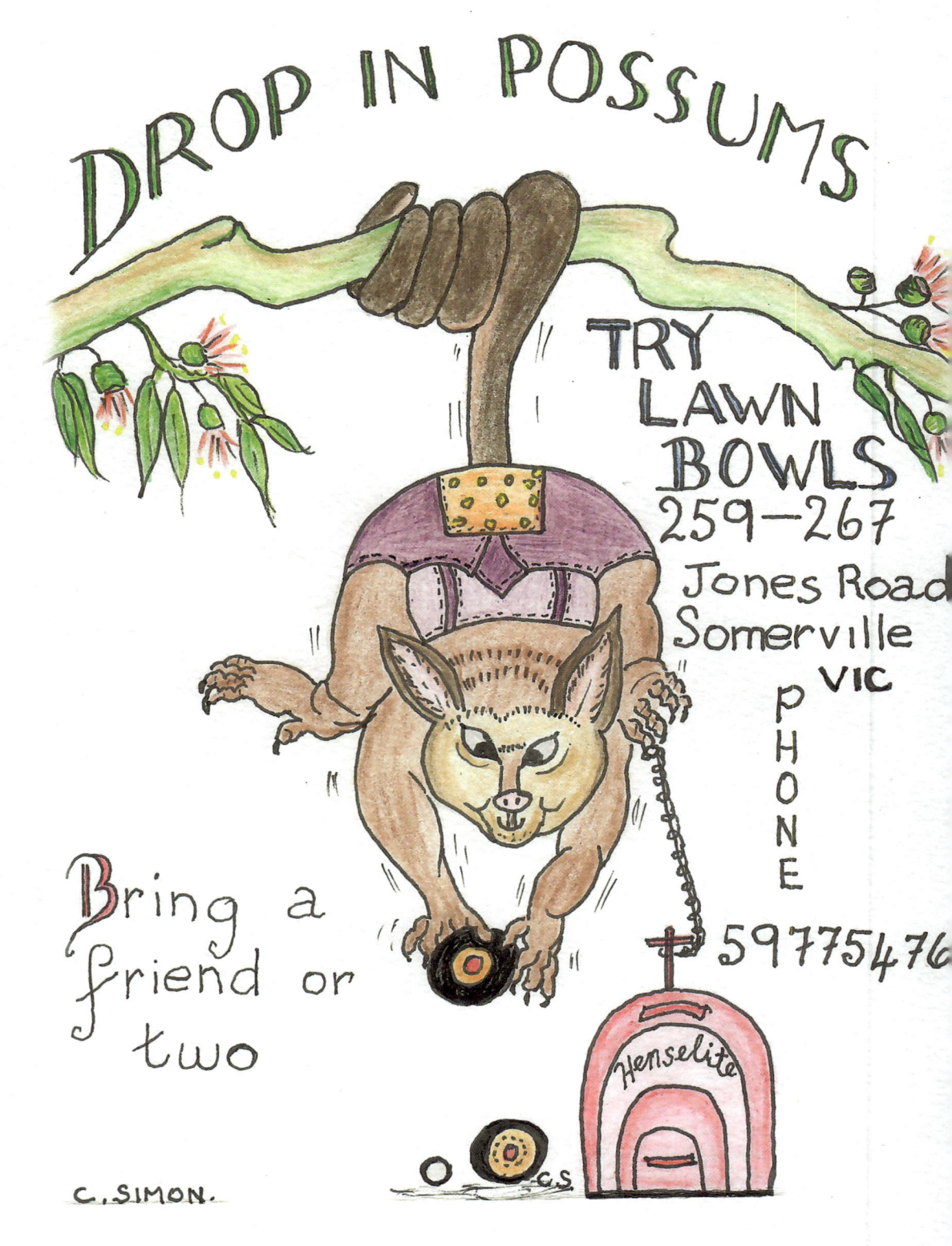

TRY LAWN BOWLS

259-267 Jones Road
Somerville VIC

PHONE 59775476

Bring a friend or two

C. SIMON.

YCJCYTDTTRFDS

– *Ross Porter*

In the bar at the Birdsville Pub in 2015, after visiting the "3 Corners", Cameron, Hadens, & Poepells, I was confronted with a notice.... "YCJCYTDTTRFDS"

Now I knew it had something to do with the RFDS, but be blowed what it meant or how to figure it out, so, I asked the barman.

His response was, "Sure mate, I can tell ya what it means, but it'll cost ya"

I glumly said "Sure mate, what's the cost?"

He said "Just a note". Then he proceeded to enlighten me and all in the bar who were unsure whether to ask a dumb question or not.

Ears were turned to the barman...

YCJCYTDTTRFDS is an acronym for "Your Curiosity Just Caused You To Donate To The Royal Flying Doctor Service"

Dumbfounded, and laughing my guts out, I took a note out of my wallet and dropped it into the RFDS tin, along with all those in the bar who were stretching their ears to hear as well.

The Birdsville Pub are great ambassadors for the RFDS!

William Creek Pub

About 30 years ago we visited the outback pub at William Creek in South Australia. It was an awesome place that supported the RFDS. The sign behind the bar was YCJCYADFTRFDS.

We couldn't work out what it meant so we asked the barman.

He said 'give me a dollar and I'll tell you' he then threw the dollar into an enormous bra hanging from the ceiling and said "your curiosity just cost you a dollar for the RFDS."

He also sold drawing pins for 20c for you to pin anything to any wall, and 20c to borrow a marker pen to write or draw on any wall. **The sign over the bra said – throw your donations in here.**

We had loads of fun while making our donations.

– *Doreen Harrison*

Mask Up

– Patricia Bish

You save a lot on lipstick
When a mask you must be wearing
Your alluring air of mystery
Will have some people staring

A fetching floral mask
Disguises many sins
Your wrinkled skin and hairy chin
And all those senior things

A deft touch of mascara
And your eyes will cause sensation
And people may not even spot
Your macular degeneration.

If you're a crafty person
And exceptionally thrifty
You could design yourself a mask
Both becoming and quite nifty

To cover up your sagging neck
Your ill-fitting false teeth...
And if you make it long enough
EVERYTHING beneath

So let us make the best of it
As our clever masks we doff
And what a shock it's going to be
When we have to take them OFF!

Breaking a Salt Lake Surface

My father Ron Hipwell first introduced me to the RFDS during the 1930s. He would take me out to their base in Broken Hill, and let me sit there and pedal like mad to generate power for their radios. They used the beautiful Dragon Rapide Aircraft for their flights at that time.

Later in life, my wife, Mary, and I moved to Port Augusta, South Australia to live and stayed there for 57 years. I became involved with Port Augusta Airport and also the RFDS were stationed there. In those days, Silver City Air Taxis, Broken Hill had the contract for RFDS flights and they used 180 Cessnas for service work. I maintained the dirt airstrip and refuelled their planes from 44 gallon drums of aviation fuel.

I have so many stories to share. One great one is on a flight, with a patient aboard, an RFDS pilot landed in the middle of Lake Torrens, during a dust storm. It was a smooth landing on a salt lake but when he stopped the plane's weight broke the salt surface and the plane sunk to half way up the undercarriage. It took us nearly 3 weeks to rescue the aircraft from the lake!

— *Brian Hipwell*

Team K9

My dad, John Gorman, goes on the Outback Car Trek every year, for the last 26 years.

I wanna nominate him or put his name down as he has been raising money for the Flying Doctor for all those years!!

I want him to be recognized with his amazing work.

This year his team (which now consist of 10 people and 3 cars) will raise upwards of 40 thousand dollars all for the Flying Doctor.

He started this! And plus his car is one of a kind – Team 9k9. Big dog and also we have the pup and the mutt.

Whenever he goes to country towns visiting the small schools he always gets the whole school on the bonnet of Big Dog. I have so many incredible photos of dad and his cars to share!

– Amy Gorman

– C.Simon

Nana Peate's Gourmet Sandwiches

— Thomas Barratt

As a young impressionable ten year old I walked into the kitchen of our semi-rural home in Dural, back in 1980.

Nana Peate was staying with us and insisted on doing the food preparation. Small in stature and frail Nana Peate was a lady in her early seventies.

Nana Peate looked at me with a brutally frank stern look in her eyes and asked "Was that you last night wandering around like a blue tail fly?" I insolently replied no.

In a bygone era before microwaves and our TV dinners cooking was a slow and more arduous process. Looking at the Duracil Floor Wax and condensed milk on the kitchen bench I then opened the fridge door and saw not much to eat. Nana said, "Your mother hasn't done her shopping, don't get your knickers in a knot, it's Thursday night shopping night."

Rather damaged by the lack of food to eat I decided to scam a bit of money for tuckshop. "Mum said we could have money for tuckshop today." Nana Peate swatted a blowfly and replied, "And pigs fly backward on Sundays," and started to spread condensed milk on our sandwiches and replied, "Don't complain, it's more than we got in the Great Depression."

Later, I was at school at lunchtime in the playground. Me and other students sat down to our lunches and began to open our bags. The other students had more interesting sandwiches and condiments to eat.

I began to chew on my sandwich and noticed it tasted a bit funny so I opened it up. "Stone the crows and pickle my grandmother, Nana Peate's put Duracil Floor Wax on my condensed milk sandwiches and what's worse, there's a squashed blowfly swimming in the 'condensed milk'!"

–Verna Hay, Gympie CWA

I moved to a cattle property in Taroom, in central Queensland, when I was first married back in 1956. It was just 15,000 acres – a small family holding really. We didn't have any way of keeping meat – there was no electricity, only a small kerosene fridge – so we had to salt everything. But when the children, Penelope, Roderick and Ivan, were young, well, you couldn't give them, salted meat all the time. They needed something fresh, something you could make a gravy with or a stew or casserole. So every now and then I would get my husband Duncan to kill a roo. He'd skin it and take out the loin chop for his casserole. The children loved it. I used to grow my own vegetables – beans, carrots, turnips and cabbages – and I would just go and pick what I wanted.

Bush Casserole

Kangaroo loin
Flour, seasoned with salt and pepper
Oil or dripping
1 onion, chopped
Vegetables
½ cup stock
Potatoes, thickly sliced

Preheat oven to 170°C.

Cut the loin into chops. Dust with seasoned flour and lightly brown in oil or dripping. Place chops in a casserole dish.

Lightly cook onion and add to casserole with any vegetables available, such as carrot, turnip (diced if large) or peas. Add stock and cover with sliced potato.

Cover and cook for about 2 hours. Can be cooked in a camp oven.

Deathly Ill Child

In April, 1982 we moved from Serpentine to the Ravensthorpe Shire in southern Goldfields-Esperance region of Western Australia. Shortly after our eldest son Bruce, aged seven years, was diagnosed with Hodgkin's Lymphoma, which required immediate attention at tertiary hospitals in Perth.

We had to significantly re-organise our daily lives.

My husband looked after the farm and the two younger sons, Charles (6 years) and Christopher (nearly 2), while I took Bruce for medical treatment. It was constant trips to and from Perth, either by car or by coach.

The doctors were excellent, – their attention to his illness and wellbeing saved his life.

On the 15th December, 1982, Bruce (who never complained) came home on the school bus and said he had a bad headache and didn't feel well. I attended to him and said it could possibly be caused by the very hot weather that day, and tiredness that comes with the end of school year.

With no improvement by the next morning I made an appointment with Dr. Dick Roberts, the resident doctor in Ravensthorpe (65 km from home). Dr. Roberts, was well aware of Bruce's condition,

– Phyllis Muller

"Our eldest son Bruce, aged seven years, was diagnosed with Hodgkin's Lymphoma."

checked him, then, without a word to me, picked up the phone and rung the RFDS in Kalgoorlie, requesting an aircraft to transport a child with Amoeba Meningitis. This was dreadful news to my ears.

I called my husband and he brought me a small overnight bag with necessary items. It was late afternoon and the local ambulance drove us to the Ravensthorpe airport. I remember waiting only a few minutes and saw the lights of the approaching aircraft in the fading sunshine.

The Royal Flying Doctor Service pilot gave us a smooth trip to Jandakot airport, and the nurse on board was very attentive, kind & caring in her duties.

Arriving at Jandakot the RFDS staff relinquished their duties over my son, for which I thanked them, and then there was an ambulance trip to hospital where Bruce was admitted for 6 days. Although Bruce was very poorly and he lost a lot of weight, his illness turned out to be viral meningitis, which with care he recovered from.

My young son is now 43 years old. Thank you to the many doctors, ambulance staff and the Royal Flying Doctor Service.

Who Done It?

When me prayers were poorly said
Who tucked me in me widdle bed
And spanked me till me arse was wed

Me Mudder

Who took me from me cozy cot
And put me on the ice cold pot
And made me pee if I could not

Me Mudder

And when the morning light would come
And in me crib me dribble some
Who wiped me tiny widdle bum

Me Mudder

Who would me hair so neatly part
And hug me gently to her heart
Who sometimes squeezed me till me fart

Me Mudder

Who looked at me with eyebrows knit
And nearly had a king size fit
When in me Sunday pants me shit

Me Mudder

When at night her bed would squeak
Me raised me head to have a peak
Who yelled at me to go to sleep

Me Farver...

So We Have Faith

At the time (approximately 20 years ago) our family – husband, self, and two young children, were living in the small remote mining community of Pannawonica in Western Australia – picture the WA coast and go about halfway up to Karratha, and then 200 kilometres south and inland is Pannawonica. Pannawonica had a Medical Centre with nursing staff, but no resident doctor in town.

Our daughter, Faith, came home from Primary School this particular day and wasn't feeling so well. As the afternoon wore on she felt worse and eventually collapsed on the back lawn. We rang the Medical Centre; they immediately dispatched the ambulance to gather her up. They monitored her (as is protocol) at the Medical Centre for the following few hours; by about 8pm that evening her vital statistics had dropped to a 'cut-off' level where they had to contact the Flying Doctor for help. There was a plane in the air returning from Perth to Port Hedland, and so it was diverted to call into Pannawonica to pick-up Faith.

The arrival time of the plane was about an hour away, and so we all did a mad rush around to pack bags and get out to the local air-strip to meet the plane. It was dark by this time.

As was necessary at that point in time, the Emergency Services Team from the mine were summoned to do a patrol run of the air-strip as it wasn't fenced then against wildlife (it subsequently has been). So we all lined up at the gate to the air-strip waiting for the plane to arrive: Emergency Services; the ambulance; and our family (I was to accompany Faith on the flight). The Emergency Service people did their 'roo run' to clear the air-strip, and were back behind the gate waiting for the plane to land (it is protocol to be behind the gate for landing).

The plane could be heard approaching – such a welcome sound and sight when you have an sick child.

It came in to touch-down and land, then all of a sudden 'BANG' and a sheet of flames – then deadly silence!!

The Emergency Service men and my husband walked down the air-strip to see whatever had happened. They found the doctor, nurse, and pilot walking up the air-strip. The plane had hit two kangaroos when beginning its touch-down to the runway; had been damaged, and was now going nowhere!! So much for the 'roo run' done previously.

Faith ended up having a Flying Doctor and a nurse, at her total disposal for the night – and she ended up only having a bout of gastritis!! The doctor, nurse, and pilot ended up staying the night in town until they could get out on another plane the next day. The poor young doctor – it was his first day on the job – got a real understanding of the damage a couple of large kangaroos can

> **"The plane could be heard approaching – such a welcome sound and sight when you have an sick child."**

> **"It came in to touch-down and land, then all of a sudden 'BANG' and a sheet of flames – then deadly silence!!"**

do to a plane! Substantial damage was done (approximately $250,000 worth we were told later).

The plane had to have a new propeller and new engine flown up from Perth. A crane from the mine had to be requisitioned to lift the old ones off and the new ones into place. So every time there was a local Flying Doctor fundraiser we Puttman's came in for some flak – "Come on; buy up big; you have a lot of damage to pay for!!" That sort of thing.

To end this story, going back ten years earlier, at the time I was pregnant with Faith, I was living in Broken Hill in outback New South Wales. I was managing a school children's hostel for The Bush Church Aid Society – 20 children each year from outback stations and towns would come and live at the hostel during school terms and go to the local schools. I had quite a large staff to help me.

Anyway, when I was seven months pregnant I went for my fortnightly doctor's check-up. I walked in and the doctor didn't even examine me – he just took one look at me and said, "We need to have you on a Flying Doctor plane out of here within the hour." All this pregnancy thing was totally new to me – I didn't know I had Toxemia – I knew I had blue swollen legs, but that was alright – I was used to being on my feet and hadn't thought anything of it.

So back to the hostel to quickly pack my bag and within the hour I was on that damned plane and headed off to Adelaide to have my first child.

Faith has been a delight ever since, and we wouldn't be without her. She's now aged 28 years, and a very competent tour guide throughout the UK and Europe, working for Contiki Tours. But, we refer to her as 'The Flying Doctor Baby' who made her way into the world two months early after a Flying Doctor flight to Adelaide, where she was born at the Flinders Medical Centre, and spent the next month in the Neonatal Unit there.

I might add, just to top off this story, as well as paid staff, we had various volunteers help at the Bush Church Aid Hostel mentioned above that I was managing. Rita Elliott (and her husband, Ron) were long standing volunteers there, and Rita was also a very, very, very long-term employee of the Royal Flying Doctor Service base at Broken Hill. She was a great advocate of the Flying Doctor and went well out of her way to always promote the Service.

Well done Rita for your efforts with The Bush Church Aid Society, and the Royal Flying Doctor Service. We loved you and Ron back then, and we still do today.

I'm attaching a photo of Faith the next morning standing beside the damaged plane at Pannawonica. The bandage on her arm is where they had put in an IV drip the night before.

– May Puttman

> **"The poor young doctor – it was his first day on the job – got a real understanding of the damage a couple of large kangaroos can do to a plane!"**

– C.Simon

Strong Australia

— Tahlia Potter

This photo reminds me much of my early years, visiting my cousins and feeding the cattle, and now as I am a teenager, it reminds me how strong Australia is, how beautiful she stands and how grateful we should be that we have people like The Flying Doctors to be on hand when we need them most.

Comic Strip

Fortunately neither I nor any of my family has ever needed the great service provided by the RFDS.

I first became aware of the RFDS when it appeared as a comic strip in the Melbourne Sun in the 1960s.

I became interested in aeroplanes at an early age and after becoming an avid reader of the comic strip, I received a Flying Doctor Annual as a present. I still have that book safely stored and these are a couple of pictures from it.

— Nick Duyvestyn

Index

Art

A Different Side to Australia	76
Drop in Possums	108
Birds	112
Knitting	122
Strong Australia	123

Poems

The Flying Doctor	01
All Dressed Up	16
Nana Peate's Curried Prawns, Circa 1974	17
Not Too Late	32
Help, I've Killed Michael!	40
End of an Era	48
Magda and Keith	58
Like He Can	61
When the Sun Went Down	65
The Stockman's Life	66
The Call of the Bush	77
Mask Up	110
Who Done It?	118

Recipes

Quick Mix Apple Cake	05
Barley Broth	24
Chicken Pie	31
Show Scones	45
Rosella Jam	55
Butterscotch Pie	56
Esmeralda Rolls	95
Bush Casserole	115

Stories

Something is Not Quite Right...	02
Only In The Bush...	03
Ten Pound Pom	06
Stinky Cloves	08
Breathe Easier	09
Old Pop	10
Memorable Flight	11
Antique Aircraft Pilgrimage	12
An Endless Sea of Stars	18
Flash Flood And No Phone!	21
Tribute to Winifried Violet Crisp	22

Just Too Long	25	Run-Way on Fire	75
My Life Line	26	Another Day at the Office...	78
Bogged in Pentland!	28	Volunteering for the RFDS	82
I Remember the Fires at Take-Off	30	Grateful	84
Indebted	35	Twice Lucky	86
Budgie Explosion	36	Broke My Back	88
Not a Matter of if, But a Matter of When	37	Under the Wing	89
"Doc" Sims	38	First Responder Uncle Herb	90
Family Cook at 8 Years	41	Service for Travellers	92
Reflections	42	Saving Reverend John Flynn	93
Nullabor Challenge	43	Help From Strangers	94
Technical Problem	46	First Flight as a Locum RFDS Medical Officer, 1966	96
Tribute to Nancy Bird (Walton)	47	Miracles Do Happen	100
King Island Resident for 50 Years	50	Remote Northern Territory in the 60s	102
A Glint of Silver in the Sky	52	Nubblegum	103
Power House Manager	57	Struth – This Can't Be Real!	104
Biscuit Tin	59	YCJCYTDTTRFDS	109
Mother-Daughter Get-Away	62	William Creek Pub	109
Grasshopper Feast	64	Breaking a Salt Lake Surface	111
Wedding Bells	68	Team K9	112
Donation	69	Nana Peate's Gourmet Sandwiches	113
Southern Cross	69	Deathly Ill Child	116
The Relief Is Palpable	70	So We Have Faith	119
My Husband's Double Injury	72	Comic Strip	123
That Feeling	74		